D0456010

My Left Foot

My Left Foot

SHANE CONNAUGHTON *and*
JIM SHERIDAN

faber and faber
LONDON · BOSTON

First published in 1989
by Faber and Faber Limited
3 Queen Square London WC1N 3AU
Reprinted 1990 (twice)

Filmset in Monophoto Plantin
Printed in England by
Clays Ltd, St Ives plc

Screenplay © Granada Television 1989
Introduction © Jim Sheridan 1989
Photographic stills © Jonathan Hession 1989
Permission to publish the screenplay *My Left Foot*
granted by Mary Brown

My Left Foot (screenplay) was based on Christy Brown's
autobiography *My Left Foot* originally published by
Secker and Warburg Limited, London

A CIP record for this book is available from the British Library

ISBN 0-571-14301-6

CONTENTS

I first met Christy Brown in 1981 when I was directing a play based on his early life. Christy came to watch a run-through. After the performance the life of the theatre got back to normal. The cleaning lady and the delivery man set about their work. I asked Christy what he thought of the young actor playing himself. I had never spoken to him before so I was not ready for the volcano that erupted. He set his mouth to speak, which was a little more difficult than usual because he had had a few drinks. To get the words out to somebody who was not used to his way of speaking was an extraordinary effort for him. He set his mouth and turned his chin to the side and down a little, so that the words seemed to spring from some primal source – and yet, at the same time, the effort to produce sound for Christy was like a machine clicking into place, all the muscles needing expert coordination. His back molars crunched off each other and the sound was jarring and eerie. All activity in the theatre stopped. The cleaning lady looked up to see where the noise was coming from; the man doing the deliveries leaned his bread on the back of a seat and looked in our direction, puzzled. I waited for the words to follow and they did, spat out like weapons. What he said was fairly simple – 'It's like the picture of Dorian Gray.' Once he stopped, the breadman moved on, the cleaning lady knocked the seat back into place, and I looked at Christy, aware that I was in the presence of a huge life.

Seven years later, I am finishing the film of *My Left Foot* and we are dubbing in Ardmore Studios outside Dublin. Daniel Day Lewis steps up to the microphone. I am shocked by the sound he produces. It has the same animal-like quality as Christy's. It jumps and ploughs through the impossible hurdles and fences set in its path. In the projection room, a face comes to the little window, looking into our world. He looks for a moment and than makes way for another. They are entranced by the voice of 'Christy' and I am transported back to that afternoon in the theatre.

I only met Christy that one time and yet something

stayed with me, or rather, something was conveyed to me – energy, trapped, seeking release. Seven years after that meeting I am flying back to Dublin from Canada. We have been having problems with the second part of the script. I get all my notes together to see what I can do. Suddenly, I am possessed by an urgent order: write. Where it comes from I do not know, but I start with a biro and the scenes start to flow really fast. Then the biro runs out of ink, so I lean across the aisle and beg a woman for a pen. On and on the writing goes. When we get into Shannon, I have almost fifty pages of script, including the scene in the restaurant, with which I am particularly happy. I don't know why this happened. I know the feeling is as if I was close to death, as if a trapped energy was being released.

Films possess a simplicity of form so that you can write in a naïve way as if the story has never been told before. In this films resemble *seanchai* – Irish mythic tales with happy endings. It makes absolute sense to me when a Hollywood mogul says to me, 'Tell me a story'. He listens and reacts on a primal level, not on an intellectual one. Surely that is the way the old fairy- and folk-tales developed: by repetition, seeing which bits worked, keeping them and polishing them. This is not necessarily condescending to the listener, for the tellers or listeners worried little about why the stories worked; they were just glad that they did. They performed the kind of function that modern analysis performs, of speaking about the unspeakable in an acceptable way. The story-tellers were telling tales that connected at a primal level and for me that is what the best films do. Like fairy-tales, you can enjoy them over and over. So, while it is true that they need a structure or battle plan, they need the magic we associate with fairy-tales even more.

Noel Pearson, the producer of the film, knew Christy a lot longer than I did. He was fascinated by Christy and his writing. They were born within a couple of hundred yards of each other in the Crumlin area of Dublin. Noel, for a time, became Christy's agent and after Christy's death, became obsessed with recording his memory. He bought the rights to his autobiographical book, *My Left Foot*, and asked myself and Shane Connaughton to come up with a screenplay. When we started working on the outline I told

Shane, 'This will be made.' Noel has that child-like enthusiasm that you can't say 'no' to. We began the script in June 1987 and started shooting in July 1988. This is phenomenally fast in the movie business and it was due in no small part to the fact that we sent the manuscript through the post to Daniel Day Lewis. When he read it, he became fired with an unbelievable enthusiasm to make it. I flew to London to meet him and our discussions were unorthodox, to say the least. Noel was almost in despair when I said that I didn't care if I directed it, so long as Daniel played Christy. Daniel, on the other hand, went against all advice to work with me on the film and committed himself to making it immediately. He had six months before his next project, so Noel had two months to raise the necessary finance. Four weeks later we were coming down to serious deadlines and Noel was seeing a lot of red ink from the bank. I called Daniel and told him that it didn't look good. 'We're making this picture,' he said, 'I'll be in Dublin tomorrow.' So Daniel came to Dublin on that Saturday and began work on the film.

During the filming there was not a cross word between me and any of the actors. The way was led by Daniel's unbelievable commitment which everyone then tried to match. Hugh O'Conor, the boy playing young Christy, at first had a particularly hard time, but after he watched Daniel he began to approximate the same reactions, and displayed the same ability with his eyes that Daniel had shown. In this regard, Gene Lambert helped a lot. Before each take he would work with Hugh, compressing into a few minutes what it had taken Daniel months to learn. I used what I knew from my own family background when directing the family scenes, and I was helped enormously by the sisters and brothers of Christy who also had small parts in the film. Lastly, I learned a great deal from the late Ray McAnally, who played Christy's father, and will be eternally grateful to him.

Jim Sheridan
July 1989

My Left Foot was first shown at the Curzon Mayfair Cinema on 18 August 1989. The cast included:

CHRISTY	Daniel Day Lewis
MR BROWN	Ray McAnally
MRS BROWN	Brenda Fricker
MARY	Ruth McCabe
DR EILEEN COLE	Fiona Shaw
OLDER BENNY	Eanna McLiam
OLDER SHEILA	Alison Whelan
OLDER TOM	Declan Croghan
YOUNGER CHRISTY	Hugh O'Conor
Lighting Cameraman	Jack Conroy
Art Director	Austen Spriggs
Editor	J. Patrick Duffner
Music	Elmer Bernstein
Costumes	Joan Bergin
Stills	Jonathan Hession
Production Manager	Mary Alleguen
Producer	Noel Pearson
Director	Jim Sheridan

INT. CHRISTY'S SHED. DAY
*1960. A foot moves in silence to a rack of records. With its
big toe and the one next to it, it removes a record from the
rack. Turns it round to have a look –* Don Giovanni *by*
Mozart. *Expertly the foot takes the actual record from the
sleeve and takes the vinyl from the internal wrapper. The
foot then places the record on a moving turntable and lifts
the needle ever so gently and places it down on the record.
Then the foot with lightning speed stops the record spinning.*

Close up: The face of CHRISTY BROWN, *a man of twenty-
eight years. He appears normal. His eyes are closed. A bead
of sweat makes its way down his large forehead. He removes
his foot from the record and almost immediately the music
begins.* CHRISTY *opens his eyes. They are bright and intense.
The music continues through the following scenes.*

EXT. DUBLIN. DAY
*The aria intensifies as a large white Rolls-Royce makes its
way through a city-centre street. People on the pavement
stand and watch. A second Rolls-Royce follows the first. The
absence of cars is noticeable, travellers mostly using bicycles.
At a traffic light the Rolls stops beside an old Ford. The two
big cars make their way to the Dublin suburbs. Now the
streets are narrower. A few children watch the cars passing.*

INT. MRS BROWN'S ROOM. DAY
MRS BROWN, *a woman in her fifties, listens to the opera.
She is immaculately dressed. She is trying on one of two
elegant hats in a mirror.*

INT. DOWNSTAIRS LIVING ROOM. DAY
*A row breaks out over mirror space in a small back room.
There are about fifteen people trying to get ready to go out.
There are three small children, four kids, three teenagers and
five adults. There is a jovial good humour despite the hectic
activity and lack of space.* BENNY *has a Teddy Boy suit on.*
TOM: You're not wearing that.

BENNY: What?
TOM: That suit. This is posh, Benny, posh.

EXT. DUBLIN STREET. DAY
*A group of children stands waiting in a cul-de-sac. It is a
poor part of Dublin. Neighbours stand out at doors talking to
each other. Suddenly the children all run to the end of the
street. Neighbours pour from their houses. The aria intensifies as
the two Rolls-Royces turn the corner like magnificent swans
in the midst of the poorly dressed children. The two Rolls-
Royces pull up outside the window with the children all cheering.*

INT. CHRISTY'S SHED. DAY
*A hand takes the needle from the record. The music stops
abruptly.* MRS BROWN *looks at* CHRISTY. *She has a formal
dinner-jacket in her hand.*
MRS BROWN: I've got to dress you, Christy.
    (*We see* MRS BROWN *start to dress* CHRISTY. *She pulls
    him forward in his wheelchair and takes off his coat and
    shirt.*)

EXT. CHRISTY'S HOUSE. DAY
*A chauffeur knocks on Christy's door. The children start to
chant, 'Christy, Christy, Christy.'*

INT. CHRISTY'S SHED. DAY
MRS BROWN: You have to wear this.
    (*A dicky bow.* CHRISTY *turns away.*)
    For my sake, Christy.
    (CHRISTY *holds his head up.* MRS BROWN *starts to put
    on the dicky bow.*)
    You've enough drink taken now, Christy, do you
    understand?
    (*The knocking intensifies at the door.*)
    Will nobody answer that door?
    (*She leaves the room.* CHRISTY *lifts a tea cosy with his
    toes. Underneath is a bottle of whiskey with a straw in
    it.* CHRISTY *sucks on the straw.*)

EXT. CHRISTY'S HOUSE. DAY
Children are milling around the door chanting, 'Christy,

Christy, Christy.' CHRISTY *emerges, being pushed in the wheelchair by his mother, and there is a magnificent cheer.* CHRISTY *smiles. His mother pushes him to the Rolls and the kids all surge forward to clap* CHRISTY *on the back. When they get to the car Christy's brother* TOM *lifts him from the wheelchair and puts him on the back seat of the car.* MRS BROWN *joins them and then Christy's brothers and sisters get into the second Rolls. All, including* BENNY, *are in formal attire.*

INT. ROLLS: THE BROWN'S STREET. DAY
TOM: It's like a royal wedding, Christy.
    (*There is a silence in the Rolls now as it leaves the children behind. Christy's mother looks at* CHRISTY *and gives him a smile of support.*)

EXT. CASTLE GROUNDS. DAY
A Punch and Judy show. We hear the sound of the swazzle of Punch's demented voice roaring, 'That's the way to do it', as he whirls a baby round and round and flings him out of the window. All the children roar with laughter.
    The face of LORD CASTLEWELLAND, *the eccentric Lord of Kilruddery. There is the hint of a smile on his face and a sadness in his eyes as he looks at the children. It is not apparent that any of them are handicapped.*
    Punch is telling another lie and insisting he is telling the truth. LORD CASTLEWELLAND *leads the children in their chant against him.*
    A hand on LORD CASTLEWELLAND's *shoulder. He looks at the servant and seems to be in a private war with Punch, talking to himself as he walks away.*

EXT. CASTLE GROUNDS. DAY
The Rolls coming down the drive and up to the front door.
LORD CASTLEWELLAND *comes to greet* CHRISTY.

INT. CASTLE: LOBBY/STAIRS. DAY
The Brown family and LORD CASTLEWELLAND
come into the lobby.
LORD CASTLEWELLAND: Welcome to my humble abode.
    (CHRISTY *smiles at him.*)
    Exactly.

3

(CHRISTY *looks up and sees a nurse,* MARY, *descend the stairs.*)

MARY: Hello, my name is Mary. I'm looking after Christy for the evening.
(*There is a big smile on* CHRISTY'*s face, as* MARY *is very pretty.*)
I have to take him to the Wellington Room.

MRS BROWN: Are you sure you'll be able to look after him on your own?

MARY: I'll be OK.

TOM: (*Shouts*) I wouldn't be too sure of that.
(MARY *wheels him away.*)
Be careful of that fellow!
(LORD CASTLEWELLAND *leads the Brown family towards the orangery.*)

INT. WELLINGTON ROOM. DAY
CHRISTY *is wheeled into the Wellington Room, which serves as a green room. He hears the noise of the audience gathering, coming from a Tannoy outside.*

CHRISTY: I need a light.

MARY: What?

CHRISTY: (*Brusque*) I need a light.

MARY: I don't smoke.

CHRISTY: I need a light.

MARY: I'm not deaf. I can hear you. You need a light. I have no matches so you're going to wait until I go out of here and get one. Don't think I'm your mother just because I'm looking after you.

CHRISTY: I don't need a fucking psychology lesson. I just need a light.

MARY: I'll get you one.
(*She leaves. Quick as a flash* CHRISTY *extracts a bottle of whiskey from his wheelchair, opens it with his teeth, puts it on the table and then gets a straw with his mouth from his top pocket. He puts the straw in and takes a large draught. He hears* MARY *coming back, whips the bottle off the table and spits out the straw.*)
Light. (*She puts the matches on the table.*) Is there anything else I can do for you?
(CHRISTY *stares at her. His intentions are clear.*)

4

I'll get you a glass. (*She gets a glass, puts it on the table.*) No point in drinking out of a bottle.
(CHRISTY *smiles at her. She pours some whiskey into a glass.*)
Do me a favour, Christy, don't get drunk. Have a drink but, for your mother's sake, don't get drunk.
CHRISTY: I'm all right.
(*There is a silence. They sit looking at each other.*)
Have I met you somewhere?
MARY: Probably.
CHRISTY: You're all right.
(*He is well on.*)
MARY: Thanks.
(*There is a long pause. They look at each other.*)
Do you have a drink problem?
CHRISTY: Yeah, I can't get enough.
MARY: I heard that one before. You don't have to be an alcoholic to be a great writer. What age are you?
CHRISTY: What age are you?
MARY: I asked you first.
CHRISTY: You sound like a kid.
MARY: I'm twenty-seven.
CHRISTY: I'm twenty-eight. Do I look it?
MARY: You wrote a book?
CHRISTY: Ah, it's all right.
MARY: I heard it was great. I'd love to read it.
CHRISTY: (*Tired and indistinct*) They are going to read it later?
MARY: What [*did you say*]?
CHRISTY: Later. Read.
MARY: I won't be here. My job's over when you go out on the stage.
CHRISTY: Stay.
MARY: (*Defensive*) I've an appointment.
CHRISTY: Another cripple?
MARY: No, as a matter of fact it's not. Why are you so aggressive?
(*Pause.*)
CHRISTY: (*Low*) I'm my father's son.
MARY: What?
CHRISTY: Nothing.

5

(*The Tannoy goes strangely silent.* CHRISTY *and* MARY *look at it. Suddenly a burst of sustained applause is heard from it.*)

INT. ORANGERY. DAY

LORD CASTLEWELLAND *stands at the end of the orangery before the seated and expectant guests.*

LORD CASTLEWELLAND: Welcome, ladies and gentlemen, to this benefit in aid of cerebral palsy. I won't ask you to put your hand in your pockets – till later. (*Laughter.*) We are going to begin the entertainment with a piano recital by Brian O'Connor and please don't accompany him with your champagne glasses.

INT. WELLINGTON ROOM. DAY

CHRISTY *looks at* MARY.

MARY: Do you want to go out and watch?

CHRISTY: (*Nervous*) No.
    (*There is an awkward silence.*)
    Would you like to see the original?

MARY: Of your book?

CHRISTY: Yeah.

MARY: I'd love to.

CHRISTY: It's a bit sentimental.

MARY: What does that mean?

CHRISTY: Ah, nothing. I wouldn't be good company. I'm tired.
    (*He lifts himself out of the chair as best he can with his arms.* MARY *removes the tattered, dog-eared manuscript from his wheelchair seat. She looks at it. On the cover is a picture of Christy's mother and above it the letters* MOTHER.)

MARY: Did you draw this?
    (CHRISTY *nods yes.*)
    It's very good.
    (CHRISTY *nods thanks. Smiles.*)
    Here, let me make you comfortable.
    (MARY *gets* CHRISTY *comfortable. She fixes his pillow. There is a certain electricity between them.* CHRISTY *closes his eyes and pretends to sleep.* MARY *tentatively turns a page.* CHRISTY *looks out of one eye.*)

6

INT. HOSPITAL. NIGHT
1932. MR BROWN *walks down the corridor of the Rotunda Hospital in Dublin. We can hear the sound of a newborn baby crying.*

INT. HOSPITAL WARD. NIGHT
MR BROWN *goes into the ward. The baby stops crying. It is visiting time. The ward is full of happy mothers and their visitors.* MR BROWN *looks for* MRS BROWN. *He can't find her. Ominously, at the end of the ward there is a curtain drawn around one of the beds.* MR BROWN *walks past it, refusing to face it. He continues to near the end of the ward and can't find* MRS BROWN. *He looks back up the ward. A nurse comes towards him and has a word with him. She points to the curtained-off bed.* MR BROWN *nods gravely.*

INT. PUBLIC HOUSE. NIGHT
MR BROWN *stands at the bar.*
MR BROWN: Give me a pint and a chaser there, Brian.
FRIEND: Congratulations.
MR BROWN: On what?
FRIEND: The new boy, Christy.
MR BROWN: Are you trying to make a jackass out of me or what? The child's an imbecile. A moron. A vegetable. I says to the doctor, 'Is there any hope for him?' and the doctor says, 'Well, Mr Brown, there is some movement in his left foot.' His left foot! He'll never be able to pick up a trowel or mend a gable wall. He's shagged good and proper.
FRIEND: You might have to put him in a home.
MR BROWN: He'll go into a coffin before any son of mine goes into a home. I'll tell you one thing though, that's the end of the road for me in the breeding stakes.
FRIEND: How will you manage that?
MR BROWN: Abstinence.
   (*Everybody looks at one another, knowing the impossibility of this.*)

INT. CHILDREN'S BEDROOM. DAY
MRS BROWN: (*Out of shot*) If you don't get up out of that bed, Tom Brown, your father will come to you.

(TOM *snores.* CHRISTY *looks at him, wide-eyed. He pulls
the clothes from him.* TOM *lazily puts his hand out and
re-covers himself.* CHRISTY *hears a foot on the stairs and
listens, startled.*)

INT. STAIRS. DAY
Close on: MR BROWN *making his way to the stairs.*

INT. CHILDREN'S BEDROOM. DAY
CHRISTY *is now lying on his back. He raises his left foot and
hits his brother an unmerciful kick in the ribs. His brother
sits up under the impact of* CHRISTY'S *blow.*
TOM: Why did you kick me, Christy Brown?
  (CHRISTY, *unable to speak correctly, grunts something
  and nods to the oncoming noise.*)
  Is that me ould fellow?
  (*He jumps out of the bed, grabs his trousers, shirt and
  shoes and dresses himself in two seconds.* MR BROWN
  storms into the room, belt drawn.)
  I'm up. I'm up, I'm up ages.
  (MR BROWN *glares at* TOM. *He leaves the room.*)
  (*Surprised*) Well done, Christy.
  (TOM *leaves the room.* CHRISTY *follows.*)

INT. STAIRS. DAY
CHRISTY *on the stairs watches* MR BROWN, BENNY, BRIAN
and SHEILA *leave the house.*

INT. LIVING ROOM. DAY
CHRISTY *goes into the kitchen and his eldest brother,* TOM, *is
wolfing down his breakfast.* CHRISTY *sits on the settee. When*
TOM *leaves, Christy's* MOTHER, *who is pregnant, stoops
down and puts her hand up the chimney. Gingerly she removes
a silver box. She shows it to* CHRISTY *and puts a pound note
into it. She then puts it back up the chimney.*
  MRS BROWN *comes over to* CHRISTY. *His eyes are on her
low-cut dress, at the top of which is a locket.* CHRISTY *is looking at her breast. She mistakes it for the locket. She opens it.*
  Close on: a couple, well dressed.
MRS BROWN: That's my mam. A princess she was, Christy.
  That's my dad, a prince charming he was.

8

(CHRISTY *closes it with his foot. He can't re-open it.*
MRS BROWN *does.*)
That was taken on holidays, Christy. HOL Y DAZE.
(*She looks sad. She starts to feed* CHRISTY *like a baby.*)
I'm going away for a little while, Christy. To hospital.
Your sisters will look after you. Do you understand?
(CHRISTY *looks apprehensive.*)
You can't be sticking to your mother like sticking
plaster, do you understand? I'll only be gone for a
few days. I better get this house ready before I go.

INT. LIVING ROOM. DAY
MRS BROWN *is polishing shoes. There are six pairs of
children's and Mr Brown's boots. She polishes away as
CHRISTY watches her, especially when she holds her back in
pain.*

INT. CHILDREN'S BEDROOM. DAY
MRS BROWN *carries* CHRISTY *and the shoes into the room
and puts* CHRISTY *on his bed. She lays the shoes out in their
proper places at the foot of each bed. She looks at* CHRISTY's
bare feet. CHRISTY *looks at them too and smiles.* MRS BROWN
*gives him a hug. Then she stands up and puts her hand to
her face and rubs her face.*
MRS BROWN: Christy. I have to go outside to make a
    phone call. You wait here.
    (CHRISTY *waits and listens to his mother on the stairs.
    There is a loud noise.*)

INT. HALLWAY. DAY
CHRISTY *on the landing. At the bottom of the stairs lies his
mother, groaning.* CHRISTY *flies down the stairs. At the
bottom of the stairs he looks at his mother, puts his foot out
to try and awaken her, but she seems unconscious. Suddenly
she lets out a huge groan and holds her stomach.* CHRISTY
*stands on one foot and leans against the banisters. He tries to
get past his fallen mother without hurting her. He flings
himself past her and lands on his head on the ground. After a
moment he starts to kick the door.*
MRS BROWN: Jesus, Mary and Joseph, where am I?
    (*She looks at* CHRISTY, *who is eyeball to eyeball with her.*)

Christy, where am I?
(*She goes unconscious again.* CHRISTY *kicks the door.*
His face throughout is a paroxysm of effort.)

EXT. STREET. DAY
Deserted. Door noise. MAGSO *putting out rubbish. She hears*
noise, goes over to the door. She looks through the letterbox.

INT. HALLWAY. DAY
Eyes through the letterbox.

INT. HALLWAY. DAY
MAGSO's *Point of view. She can see* CHRISTY *upside down.*
MAGSO: What's up, Christy?
(MAGSO *hears a moan and looks to the left of the*
letterbox, where she can see MRS BROWN *lying on the*
floor.)
Jesus, Mary and Joseph.
(*She pulls the key strings up through the letterbox and*
the door begins to open.)

EXT. STREET. DAY
CHRISTY *sits alone on the street as all the neighbours crowd*
around the house. The ambulance pulls away with Christy's
mother and CHRISTY *watches it depart.*
MAGSO: It was the grace of God that door was unlocked.
NAN: What happened?
MAGSO: She was carrying Christy down the stairs when
she fell. I heard an unmerciful bang and rushed over
to the door. Poor Christy was lying at the bottom of
the stairs like a moron.
NAN: He's an awful cross to the poor woman.
MAGSO: It's in a home he ought to be. He has the mind
of a three-year-old.

INT. LIVING ROOM. DAY
Close on: a children's reader.
MAGSO: (*From book*) A is for apple. B is for bus. C is for
car. And D is for dunce. You poor unfortunate
gobshite.
(CHRISTY *looks at* MAGSO.)

INT. KITCHENETTE. DAY
MAGSO *opens the cupboards.*
MAGSO: Will you look at that. Enough to feed an army.
You'll never go hungry anyway, Christy.

INT. CHRISTY'S HOUSE. NIGHT
Close on: a tiny baby in a cot. CHRISTY *is looking down at
her perched on the settee. In another part of the room the
younger children are doing their homework.*
MR BROWN: Twenty-five per cent of a quarter. Now that's
a stupid question. Twenty-five per cent is a quarter.
You can't have a quarter of a quarter.
SHEILA: (*Getting herself made up*) You can, can't you,
Christy?
(CHRISTY *nods yes.*)
MR BROWN: What would he know?
(CHRISTY *picks up the chalk.* TOM *looks at him.*)
SHEILA: Mam, Mam, Christy picked up the chalk.
(MRS BROWN *comes running into the room.*)
MRS BROWN: Go on, Christy, make your mark.
(CHRISTY *makes a mark on the floor. A long line.*
SHEILA *kneels.*)
SHEILA: What is it?
(CHRISTY *makes another line through it.*)
What's that, Christy?
MR BROWN: That's nothing. It's nothing. It's a squiggle.
MRS BROWN: Give him a chance.
(CHRISTY *draws another line so that the whole thing
looks like a crow's foot. He tries to redirect the chalk but
fails, he rubs it out with the heel of his foot and starts
over again. This time the line ends up crooked and* CHRISTY
hurls the chalk away.)
Well done, Christy. Here (*getting chalk*), try again.
Try to do it again.
MR BROWN: Will you stop getting notions, woman. The
child's a cripple. Face facts. It'll do nobody any good
putting quare thoughts in his head. I'm going out for
a pint.
(CHRISTY *looks up at his father. Behind his back his
mother is silently clapping* CHRISTY. *He acknowledges
the applause by nodding his head, but the father looks*

behind and catches her. He shakes his head in frustration at her stupidity.)

EXT. STREET. DAY
Coming up the road are three nuns waddling like penguins.

INT. CHILDREN'S BEDROOM. DAY
CHRISTY *sits up in bed. The door knocks.* MRS BROWN *answers. We can hear the words, 'Christy Brown', 'retarded'. He hears them come into the house and the words, 'cup of tea'.*

INT. CHILDREN'S BEDROOM. DAY
His mother comes to the door.
MRS BROWN: I want you to meet some of the Sisters, Christy.
(CHRISTY *shies away from his mother. She comes towards him, picks him up.* CHRISTY *puts his arms around her.)*

INT. LIVING ROOM. DAY
MRS BROWN *carries* CHRISTY *into the living room. She looks at her waist.* CHRISTY *has wrapped his left foot around her waist in a vice-like grip.*
SISTER: So, this is the little boy. What's your name?
(CHRISTY *says nothing.)*
Have you lost your tongue?
MRS BROWN: It's very hard to understand what he says at the best of times.
SISTER: Come on to me, Christy.
(CHRISTY *grabs on to his mother. He won't let go. He is terrified of the nuns.)*
What will he do when you're not here to help him, Mrs Brown?
MRS BROWN: He has his brothers and sisters to look after him.
SISTER: But they will want families of their own. He's not able to communicate in any way.
MRS BROWN: I understand him.
SISTER: Yes, but how will he make himself understood? Will he ever be able to make a proper confession?

12

Will he be able to make peace with his Maker when
his time comes?
MRS BROWN: Would you like a cup of tea, sisters?

EXT. CHRISTY'S HOUSE. DAY
The nuns leave the house.
SISTER: When Christy comes to stay with us we'll get a
big wheelchair for him to move around in.
(MRS BROWN *says goodbye to them and shuts the door.*
CHRISTY *still holds on to her.*)

INT. CHRISTY'S HOUSE. DAY
MRS BROWN *is setting the table for the tea. There is a knock*
on the door. MRS BROWN *goes out to answer it, but finds she*
cannot move. CHRISTY *has his foot wrapped around her leg.*
MRS BROWN: Let go of my leg, Christy.
(CHRISTY *won't let go.* MRS BROWN *bends down and*
picks him up. She looks him straight in the eye.)
Don't be worried about them old nuns. Just because
they have no children of their own they come looking
for ours, but your mother is no gom, do you
understand me?
(*She winks.* CHRISTY *gives a weak smile.*)

EXT. FRONT DOOR. DAY

MR BROWN, *watched by* CHRISTY *and* MRS BROWN *and brothers and sisters, is putting the finishing touches to a go-cart, made from pram wheels and a wooden box. It looks rough but tough.*

MR BROWN: Better than any wheelchair, I'm tellin' you!

MRS BROWN: Cheaper anyway.

MR BROWN: (*Looking at her impatiently*) Put him in it.

MRS BROWN: Wait.

(*She puts a cushion in the box. Then she lifts* CHRISTY *into it.*)

MR BROWN: All it needs now is the engine.

SHEILA: (*Innocent*) Are you putting an engine in it, Da?

MR BROWN: Yeah. You're the engine – the lot of youse.

(MR BROWN *and his wife watch as the children push* CHRISTY *down the street, gathering speed.*)

MRS BROWN: Go easy.

(MR BROWN *laughs.*)

EXT. STREET. DAY

All the boys are huddled over a magazine. We hear occasional voices saying, 'Look at that', and war whoops. CHRISTY *watches from his chariot, wondering why he has been forgotten.*

BOY: That's her thing. You put your thing in there for a half-hour and you get a baby.

OTHER BOY: If you do it for an hour you get twins.

(TOM *hits the boy on the head. All laugh.*)

BENNY: Here's Ma, Tom.

TOM: Oh, my God, here, it's not my magazine.

(*Nobody will take it.*)

(*Handing it to* BENNY) Hide it.

BENNY: Where?

(MRS BROWN *is almost upon them.* BENNY *grabs the magazine and puts it under* CHRISTY'S *arse in the chariot.* CHRISTY *tries to stop him but doesn't succeed.*)

MRS BROWN: Right, in for your tea, you lot.

(*She pushes* CHRISTY *in the chariot.*)

EXT. DOOR. DAY
MRS BROWN *attempts to take* CHRISTY *from the chariot.*
TOM: It's OK, Ma, we'll carry him in.
　　(BENNY *and* TOM *carry the chariot into the house.*)

INT. LIVING ROOM. NIGHT
Everybody has gone to bed. CHRISTY *is asleep in the chariot.*
His dinner on his lap.
MR BROWN: He loves that chariot.
　　(MRS BROWN *lifts* CHRISTY. *Underneath him is a dirty*
　　magazine. MRS BROWN *sees it.*)

INT. LIVING ROOM. DAY
Close on: CHRISTY *with genuine fear in his eyes.*
PRIEST: And purgatory – you understand about purgatory,
　　Christy? You can get out of the fires of purgatory but
　　never out of hell. Do you understand?
MRS BROWN: Well, Father?
PRIEST: I think it would be best if he didn't receive
　　communion for the time being, Mrs Brown.
MRS BROWN: Why, Father?

PRIEST: I don't think he would understand that it's the body and blood of Christ that he's receiving. Sure, he wouldn't know what a sin was if it hit him on the head.
(CHRISTY *appears vacant and staring.*)

INT. CHURCH. NIGHT
MRS BROWN *carries* CHRISTY *up the aisle of the church and into a seat. Scattered people at prayer.*
MRS BROWN: This is All Souls' Night, Christy. Every time you say five Our Fathers, five Hail Marys and five Glory Bes a soul flies out of the fires of purgatory and up to heaven.
(CHRISTY *vacant and staring.* MRS BROWN *is praying. People are walking in and out of the church doing their indulgences.* MRS BROWN *finishes and picks* CHRISTY *up. She walks out of the church.*)

EXT. CHURCH GROUNDS. NIGHT
MRS BROWN *tries to put* CHRISTY *into his chariot. He resists.*
MRS BROWN: What's wrong, Christy? (*She looks at him for a long time.*) Do you want to say another prayer for the poor souls?
(CHRISTY *impassive but trying to say yes.*)
Remember, Christy, even if we can't understand you, God can.

INT. CHURCH. NIGHT
CHRISTY *sits in the pew, his head against the end of the seat. From his point of view we see the huge dome of the church.*

EXT. STREET. NIGHT
MRS BROWN *pushes* CHRISTY *along in his chariot. Ahead of them is a huge bonfire. Out of the bonfire a flare shoots up to heaven.*
MRS BROWN: Look, Christy. There! There! God heard you, that's your soul flying up to heaven.
(CHRISTY *appears happy. Suddenly around a corner appears a devil-like face completely covered in black.* CHRISTY *gets scared.*)
You frightened the living daylights out of him.
TOM: Don't be scared, Christy, it's just me. Your brother Tom. (*Rubs a finger on his face*) Look, boot polish.

16

(*The bonfire blazes. A girl comes towards* CHRISTY *dressed as a witch, black teeth and a broomstick.* CHRISTY *cannot help being scared. Then* SHEILA, *his sister, appears in all the colours of the rainbow with a sun on her head. The whole scene is like something out of Bruegel.*)

INT. CHRISTY'S HOUSE. NIGHT
MRS BROWN *is hanging an apple from the ceiling. The rest of the family are eating colcannon.* SHEILA *is feeding* CHRISTY.
BENNY: I have it. I have it. (*Takes a paper from his mouth and opens it.*) A halfpenny. Last year it was a penny.
MRS BROWN: (*Low*) Keep quiet. Your father hasn't the price of a pint.

INT. CHRISTY'S HOUSE. NIGHT
CHRISTY *is trying to take a bite from the apple on the string. His attempts are grotesque and uncoordinated. The apple flies all round his face. Eventually he gives up his attempt. His father carries a basin of water into the room.* SHEILA *is now trying to get the apple. Her bosom seems exaggerated and pronounced. There is a sensuality in her attempts. Eventually she bites the apple.*

INT. CHRISTY'S HOUSE. NIGHT
MR BROWN: OK. Here's the big prize of the night. Let's see who can get the threepence out of the basin.
    (TOM *tries first.*)
TOM: It's too deep. Nobody could get that.
    (BENNY *tries and fails hopelessly.* CHRISTY *looks at his mother.*)
MRS BROWN: Let Christy try.
MR BROWN: What?
MRS BROWN: Let Christy have a go.
    (CHRISTY *puts his head in and tries. He keeps his head in for ages moving it about until he jams the threepence in against the side of the basin. Then for what seems ages he doesn't move.*)
TOM: He can't keep his head in that long.
MRS BROWN: He can keep it in as long as he likes.

(*Ages go by.*)

BENNY: I think he's drowned.

SHEILA: Get him out, Dad. Christy can't breathe good.

MRS BROWN: Leave him be.

(*Seconds elapse.*)

SHEILA: Oh no, no, he's dead, Christy is dead. (*Screams*)
He's not moving.

(*The father puts his hand out to* CHRISTY *but at the
same time he emerges from the basin like Jaws, desperate
for air, the threepence in his mouth. He leans towards
his father.*)

MRS BROWN: He wants you to have the threepence.

MR BROWN: Why?

(CHRISTY *bends his head back.*)

MRS BROWN: (*A question*) For a pint?

(CHRISTY *appears vacant.*)

EXT. FUNFAIR. DAY

CHRISTY *is carried on* TOM's *shoulders as they go through
the crowds of people at a funfair. Chocolate all over his face
and a half-eaten Toblerone in his hand. When he sees the
chair-o-planes he grunts. His brother stops and they go up the
steps to get a ride on the chair-o-planes. The* ATTENDANT
sees them.

ATTENDANT: He's not allowed on.

(MR BROWN *appears.*)

MR BROWN: Why not?

(*He looks fierce.*)

ATTENDANT: 'Cause he's a cripple.

MR BROWN: Get out of the way.

(*Frightened, he stands aside. The kids rush to the chair-
o-plane and put* CHRISTY *in the seat.*)

EXT. FUNFAIR. DAY

They try to get CHRISTY *down off the chair-o-plane but he
refuses. There is something frightening about his refusal as
if somewhere inside he realizes for the first time that he is
equal to everybody else. He stays aboard as it takes off
again.* MR *and* MRS BROWN *watch as* CHRISTY *whizzes
around.*

MRS BROWN: He's happy.

MR BROWN: Sure, it's the closest he'll ever come to being normal, woman.

INT.CHRISTY'S HOUSE. NIGHT
Everybody is sitting around. MR BROWN *is sitting reading the paper in bad humour. The children are doing their homework.* CHRISTY *is sitting there with the chalk between his toes. He has drawn a straight line. Hold on:* CHRISTY's *foot as he makes another line at a 45-degree angle to the first.*
SHEILA: Look at Christy, Mammy, He's making a triangle.
　　(CHRISTY *finishes the line, looks at everybody looking at him and then raises his foot to finish the figure. He starts halfway up one of the lines.*)
MR BROWN: He's starting in the wrong place.
　　(CHRISTY *tries to join the two lines together, but his foot gives up and it ends in a squiggle. Then* MR BROWN *takes the chalk in his hand. He draws a triangle.*)
　　Look, Christy, that's a triangle.
　　(CHRISTY *looks at him furiously. Rubs out his father's line.*)
MRS BROWN: It's not a triangle, it's an A.
　　(CHRISTY *grunts a deep strong grunt of acknowledgement. There is something primitive and territorial about it. It is his first articulation in the film. The father eyes him warily, sits back and looks at* MRS BROWN. *All the kids are watching* CHRISTY. TOM *comes through the door.*)
TOM: What's up?
MR BROWN: Keep quiet.
TOM (*Slight threat*) All I said was 'What's up?'
MR BROWN: And all I said was 'Keep quiet.'
　　(*He starts to take off his belt.*)
TOM: (*Standing*) All I said was . . .
　　(*The father lets out a primal roar.*)
MR BROWN: Sit down.
　　(TOM *sits, mesmerized and slightly embarrassed. Close on:* CHRISTY *as he watches the tribal war.* MRS BROWN *rushes from the room and comes back with some money in her hand.*)
MRS BROWN: Here.
MR BROWN: What's that?

MRS BROWN: Money. Go and have a drink.

MR BROWN: Where did you get it?

MRS BROWN: From the fairies. Go and get a drink for yourself.

MR BROWN: I don't need a drink. I just need to be obeyed in my own home.

(CHRISTY *has picked up the chalk again and is drawing on the floor again. They all watch him. He again draws the beginning of a triangle or an A. He stops when he completes two sides.*)

MRS BROWN: Go on, Christy.

(CHRISTY *starts at the outside of the second line and draws another line back up at an angle of 45 degrees.*)

MR BROWN: If that's a fucking A, I'm Adolf Hitler.

(*At the top* CHRISTY *starts back down.*)

SHARON: He's drawing another triangle.

(CHRISTY *finishes the line. They all watch him.*)

MRS BROWN: Than's an M.

(*Another deep primitive grunt from* CHRISTY. *He immediately starts on another letter. Close on: his face, and you would think he was having a baby as the sweat stands out on his brow. He draws a curious half-moon and then goes on to make a primitive O.*)

O.
(*Nobody is able to talk. All have been dumbstruck by*
CHRISTY. *He continues drawing on the floor and there is
a magical effect to the lettering, almost as if he were
discovering the letters, as if they were his own shapes
newly thought up, a strange alphabet springing from a
deep urge to communicate. He makes the T.* MR BROWN
is transfixed and mouths the word MOT. CHRISTY
*continues on and does the letter H. All the children
during the time* CHRISTY *is drawing have edged towards
the mother. Involuntarily the younger ones have put their
arms around her legs.* MR BROWN *stands alone, unaware
in the drama that he has become isolated. When* CHRISTY
draws the E, one of the kids says 'Mother', but MRS
BROWN *stops her with a raised finger, afraid that any
break in the silence will destroy the magic. The
perspiration on* CHRISTY'*s brow is translucent. He
continues drawing the R with a maniacal energy. When
he finishes he looks at the father, defiance, anger and ten
years' frustration released in a minute.* MR BROWN *is
stunned;* MRS BROWN *and all the children wait on his
reaction.* MRS BROWN *appears calm and assured, an
interior knowledge made flesh.*)
MR BROWN: Good Jesus, holy Jesus, suffering Jesus. (*Picks*
CHRISTY *up.*) You're a Brown all right.
Christy's a Brown. (*Holds him aloft like a chalice.*)
Christy fucking Brown. Give me that money, woman.
(MRS BROWN *gives him the money.*)

EXT. STREET. NIGHT
MR BROWN *carries* CHRISTY *out on to the street, followed by*
TOM *and* BENNY, *his two eldest sons. Doors start to open
and windows are pulled back to see what's going on.* MR
BROWN *stands silhouetted in the glow of a lamp.*
MR BROWN: This is Christy Brown. My son. Genius.
(*He walks on.*)

INT. PUB. NIGHT
MR BROWN *walks into the pub and plonks* CHRISTY *down on
the bar.*
MR BROWN: Give this man a drink.

(*The barman pulls a pint for the father and gives*
CHRISTY *a 7-Up.*)
Straw.
(*The barman produces a straw and the crowd
gathers round to watch* CHRISTY. *He watches them and
then bangs his foot on the table. The father doesn't know
what he wants.*)
MAN: He wants the pint.
(MR BROWN *puts the straw in the pint and* CHRISTY
drinks. It tastes awful. The crowd laugh. CHRISTY
*watches, furious, and then he gets his head down to the
straw and takes a sizeable sup. The crowd all applaud
him.* CHRISTY *beams and bangs the table with his foot.
He is part of the man's world at last.*)
MR BROWN: There's nothing wrong with this fellow.

INT. WELLINGTON ROOM. NIGHT
MARY *the nurse looks up from her book. She looks at*
CHRISTY *for a while, his head bent upon his shoulder. A
knock comes to the door and* DR COLE, *an attractive woman,
looks into the room.*
DR COLE: Is he OK?
MARY: He's fine.

DR COLE: He can get obstreperous sometimes.

MARY: No, he's been really nice. He's asleep now.

(*Close on:* CHRISTY. *One eye opens and he looks at*
MARY *and* DR COLE. *The doctor leaves and from*
CHRISTY'*s point of view we can see* MARY *move about*
the room. It is obvious from CHRISTY'*s particular*
perspective that she has a good figure and a dancer's
way of moving. She stretches to remove something from
a shelf and part of her thighs is revealed. CHRISTY *opens*
both eyes widely. MARY *turns around.* CHRISTY *closes*
his eyes just in time and moans in his 'sleep'. MARY
comes over and sits back down to read. On the page in
front of her is CHRISTY'*s face and his hair a mass of*
flames. Underneath the word HELL.)

INT. CHRISTY'S HOUSE. NIGHT

A birthday celebration for CHRISTY. *All the family is there,*
including the children we saw earlier, now grown up, TOM,
BENNY *and* SHEILA. *There are thirteen children in the family*
altogether. MRS BROWN *lights the candles. The kids call out*
the number as she lights them.

KIDS: Eleven, twelve, thirteen, fourteen, fifteen, sixteen,
seventeen.

MR BROWN: Go on now, my boy.

MRS BROWN: Christy's a man now, father. Now, Christy,
seventeen candles. Take a deep breath and blow them
all out.

(CHRISTY *struggles and grunts for breath. He is just about*
to blow them out when the baby starts crying. He stops.)

MR BROWN: Will you shut that baby up, woman.

(CHRISTY *stares at his father.* SHIELA *smiles at*
CHRISTY.)

SHEILA: Take it easy, Christy.

(CHRISTY *takes a breath but all the time watches his*
mother trying to calm the baby.)

TOM: What are you wishing for, Christy?

(CHRISTY *looks at his mother, then at his father. He starts*
to blow as hard as he can. All the family watches as he tries
to blow them out. We can see the twelve brothers and sisters
willing him on and CHRISTY *is blue-faced trying to win. He*
has to stop after nine or ten candles.)

23

BENNY: You have to do it in one go, Christy.
> (CHRISTY *tries again. All the candles go out but one,*
> *which* CHRISTY *tries to extinguish several times.*)
> It's like the bleeding fire of hell that one.
> (CHRISTY *picks up one of his birthday cards between his*
> *toes and swishes out the last candle with it. The kids*
> *cheer weakly. Then on a sign they clean the plate empty*
> *of cake.* MRS BROWN *whispers to* CHRISTY.)

MRS BROWN: Don't worry, you'll get your wheelchair.

EXT. STREET. DAY
A football match seen through a maze of iron that looks like
a prison setting. A tough, uncompromising street game. At
the far end of the pitch we can see a white goal painted on a
dark wall. Sitting in goal is CHRISTY. *One of the teenagers*
bursts through and shoots at goal. CHRISTY *in goal throws*
himself full tilt at the ball. Close on: the ball underneath
CHRISTY'*s head.*

BENNY: Well done, Christy.
> (BENNY *sits on the touchline rubbing his ankle. Another*
> *player runs on and tries to kick the ball into the net*
> *from under* CHRISTY'*s head.* TOM *immediately pushes*
> *him.* BENNY *runs from the sideline.*)

TOM: Leave his head alone.
> (*The fight subsides.* CHRISTY *is ready for action, looking fiercest of all.*)
> Free out!
> (*The game continues.* CHRISTY *watches the play. At the other end a boy handles the ball.*)

BENNY: Penno.

BOY: I'll take the penalty.

TOM: Christy's taking it.
> (*They carry* CHRISTY *the length of the pitch. They place* CHRISTY *in front of the ball.*)

GOALKEEPER: You can't hold him up.
> (TOM *and* BENNY *let* CHRISTY *go. He stands in place, writhing and squirming as everybody watches in a strange absolute silence. Close on:* CHRISTY'*s face. A paroxysm of effort. He totters and the opposing goalkeeper starts to laugh. He can't contain himself.* CHRISTY *falls but keeps his eye on the goal. The keeper is doubled up laughing and* CHRISTY *on his back lashes out with his left foot and scores. The other team berates the keeper.*)

PLAYERS: Why weren't you watching? You let a cripple beat you. You idiot.

EXT. WASTE GROUND. DAY
Corrugated iron. Chalk of a strange body. Through a hole the boys peep. A boy collects pennies. One by one the boys go behind a corner to have a look at JENNY'*s breasts.* RACHEL *sits some distance away on a wall.* BENNY *comes out from behind a wall.*

BENNY: (*To* BRIAN) You should see her knockers. Like that they are (*Making gesture*).

BRIAN: Do you want to see, Christy?

BENNY: It's only a penny, Christy.

CHRISTY: (*Inarticulate*) No!

BRIAN: It's out to there, Christy.

CHRISTY: (*Inarticulate*) No!
> (*They force his head through. The girl just looks at him. Another girl bends towards him.*)

EXT. WALL. DAY
Close on: CHRISTY'*s face through the corrugated iron.*

RACHEL: You're the nicest of the lot. Do you want to kiss
    me? There [*on the lips*]. (*She bends down and kisses*
    CHRISTY.)
    You've nice eyes.

INT. CHILDREN'S BEDROOM. NIGHT
CHRISTY *is painting. It is in the form of a love letter that he*
is doing for RACHEL. *In it* RACHEL *is idealized and*
CHRISTY *himself is part of a floating couple, perhaps like*

*Chagall or something. Magic. A moon and a heart with the
letters RB and CB with an arrow through them. Kisses and
a little poem.* CHRISTY *is painting with the aid of a bicycle
lamp. Outside a full moon. He is concentrating. It is difficult
to paint the blue in the eyes.* CHRISTY *takes the brush in his
mouth and with a huge effort paints a dot of blue. Off screen
we hear the voice of* SHEILA.
SHEILA: Ah, don't (*Giggle*), Brendan, stop. Not here. If me
    da hears us there will be murder.

EXT. STREET. NIGHT
They move into the shadow as CHRISTY *goes back to his
painting.*

INT. CHILDREN'S BEDROOM. NIGHT
*He paints the romantic scene in contrast to the occasional
noise from below.*
SHEILA: Not here, Brendan. Later.
    (CHRISTY *can't concentrate. One of his brothers snores
    in his sleep.* CHRISTY *shines the lamp round the room.
    There seem to be about ten children, boys and girls, all
    asleep in the room.* CHRISTY *knocks off the lamp and
    lies down.*)

INT. CHILDREN'S BEDROOM. NIGHT
CHRISTY *is awake. Outside the moon. Downstairs there is a
row between* MRS BROWN *and* SHEILA. *We can hear* MRS
BROWN *shout, 'Are you a good girl?'* SHEILA *replies, 'I am.
I am.'*
    Close on: CHRISTY, *wide awake, listening. We hear the
sound of the door open.* SHEILA *comes into the room. She
stands in the window looking out. She starts to take off her
clothes. When she gets to her slip and undergarments she
starts to rub her hands all over her body.* CHRISTY *watches
her. Slowly we hear his breathing getting heavier.* SHEILA
stops and looks at him.
SHEILA: Are you OK? God, you're sweating, Christy. Are
    you sick? Look at the moon, Christy, isn't it gorgeous?
    Go to sleep, Christy.

INT. CHRISTY'S HOUSE. NIGHT

MR BROWN *pushes his pay packet towards* MRS BROWN. *She looks at it.* CHRISTY *watches.*

MRS BROWN: What's this?

MR BROWN: It's holiday pay, isn't it? (*Pause.*) I'm laid off.

MRS BROWN: What about Christy's wheelchair?
    (*Close on* CHRISTY.)

MR BROWN: (*Enraged*) Christy will get his wheelchair,
    OK?

MRS BROWN: Why did you get laid off?

MR BROWN: A brick hit the foreman on the head
    accidentally on purpose.
    (*The kids laugh.*)
    And don't contradict me in front of the children, Mrs.

EXT. STREET. DAY

RACHEL *and* JENNY *with the painting and poem we saw earlier.*

JENNY: Your beautiful eyes are splendid pools of blue.
    (*Looks at* RACHEL). Yeah. In those depths I swim
    regularly. Excuse me!

RACHEL: Isn't it lovely? Like a prince, Tom Brown is.
    (*Close on: the picture of herself that* CHRISTY *painted.*)

JENNY: Let's see. (*Snatches it.*) That's not Tom. That's
    Christy. Look, CB. Christy Brown. The cripple.
    (RACHEL *is shocked.*)
    (*Taunting*) Are you in love with Christy Brown the
    cripple?

EXT. CHRISTY'S HOUSE. DAY

RACHEL *at the door.* JENNY*waits in the distance.* BENNY *answers.*

RACHEL: Can I speak to Christy Brown, please?

BENNY: Christy, you're wanted.
    (CHRISTY *comes out on his left foot, happy. His brothers
    whistle and jeer good-naturedly.*)

RACHEL: (*Showing note*) Did you paint that?
    (CHRISTY *nods yes.*)
    I can't take it. (*With pity.*) Sorry!
    (*She leaves it down gently. She goes.*)

JENNY: (*Shouting back*) Tell your brother Tom we were
    asking for him.

(CHRISTY *is annoyed.* TOM *pats him on the head but* CHRISTY *shakes his hand away.*)

INT. LIVING ROOM. NIGHT
MRS BROWN *ladles porridge into the children's plates. All thirteen of them.* MRS BROWN *is pregnant.*
TOM: What's this?
MRS BROWN: What does it look like?
TOM: But we had porridge for dinner.
MR BROWN: So?
TOM: And we had it for breakfast.
MR BROWN: (*more intense*) So?
TOM: (*Low*) I'm not eating any more.
MR BROWN: Get that into you.
TOM: I can't.
MR BROWN: Get it into you.
  (*He stands up.* TOM *eats a tiny piece.*)
  More!
  (TOM *spits it out defiantly.* MR BROWN *quickly walks round and stands beside him.* TOM *starts to eat.* CHRISTY *grunts something.* TOM *and* BENNY *look at their father. They start to snigger,* TOM *laughing through his tears.* MRS BROWN *looks at* CHRISTY *in a chastising way. She puts her hand to her breast. The locket is missing.* BENNY *and* TOM *start to snigger.* CHRISTY *grunts something low and they explode laughing.*)
  What did he say?
  (*They laugh more.*)
  What did he say, woman?
MRS BROWN: He just said the porridge is lovely.
  (CHRISTY *grunts again and the word 'bully' is almost distinct. Now the girls start to laugh.* CHRISTY *grunts again and everybody explodes.*)
MR BROWN: Keep quiet.
  (*Everybody goes quiet. Very low* CHRISTY *starts to whistle. Everybody is trying desperately not to laugh but the effort is too much.* MR BROWN *goes over towards* CHRISTY.)
  Christy Brown, keep quiet.
  (CHRISTY *goes quiet but when the father returns to the porridge* CHRISTY *whistles once and then stops.*

MR BROWN *looks at* CHRISTY *in a fury. He stands up, about to go into action. Thinks about it. Close on:* CHRISTY, *combative.* MR BROWN *looks at* CHRISTY, *smiles and then starts to laugh. He gently leaves the room.* MRS BROWN *goes over to* CHRISTY *and speaks.*)

MRS BROWN: Your father is a good man, Christy. He works his fingers to the bone trying to feed the lot of you.

INT. CHILDREN'S BEDROOM. NIGHT
CHRISTY *paints alone. The painting of hell we saw earlier. He works miraculously with his left foot. One or two kids sleep in the beds.* MRS BROWN *enters the bedroom.*

MRS BROWN: I'm sorry, Christy, but everybody has to go to bed.
(CHRISTY *grunts something.*)
I know you have to paint but there's no coal downstairs, Christy. Don't put my nerves under any more strain.
(CHRISTY *grunts, 'sorry' and lies back on the bed. The kids come into the room.*)
Some day you'll have a place of your own, Christy.

INT. CHILDREN'S BEDROOM. NIGHT
Everybody is snoring. CHRISTY *is wide awake. He listens intently. He hears the springs on a bed. Then he hears a groan. He twists and turns trying to sleep. Again he hears the springs.*

INT. CHRISTY'S HOUSE. MORNING
CHRISTY *awakes, his eyes ablaze, kicks his brothers* TOM *and* BENNY *awake.*
BENNY: What's up Christy?
    (CHRISTY *grunts a word.*)
    What?
    (CHRISTY *grunts again.*)
    Coal?
    (CHRISTY *nods assent.*)
    It's too early.
    (*He pulls the covers back up.* CHRISTY *manoeuvres them with his foot and in a spitting image of his father shouts.*)
CHRISTY: Gcoall.

EXT. STREET. DAY
TOM, BENNY *and* CHRISTY *are waiting at the canal bridge traffic lights. When the lorry stops they jump on the back of the lorry and start to steal coal. One of the men comes from the front of the lorry and almost catches* TOM. *They pick up the pieces and head off. Close on:* CHRISTY *in his chariot, thinking intensely. He calls* TOM *in his growl.* TOM *listens to* CHRISTY *as* CHRISTY *makes an upward movement with his foot and hands.* TOM *looks at* CHRISTY.
TOM: You mean on the back of the lorry?
    (CHRISTY *nods.* TOM *thinks about it and then pats* CHRISTY *on the head.*)
    Brilliant. Bleeding brilliant, Christy.

EXT. TRAFFIC LIGHTS. DAY
A lorry comes along full of coal and stops. TOM *nonchalantly walks towards the lorry. The* HELPER *leans from the lorry and shouts.*

31

HELPER: Stay off the back of that lorry or you'll get your arse kicked.

(*Close on:* TOM *as he hits a lynchpin from the back of the lorry. He then goes to the other side of the lorry and does the same. The lights change.*)

BENNY: Nothing happened.

TOM: Wait until it goes up the hill.

(*The lorry goes up the canal bridge hill and the force of the coal on the lorry door slowly tilts it open. The coal trickles out for a moment. Close on:* CHRISTY, *his face developing into an infernal grin. The trickle becomes an avalanche and soon twenty tonnes of coal is cascading out of the lorry.* CHRISTY's *face is an orgasm of pleasure.*)

EXT. STREET. DAY

CHRISTY *in his chariot, totally black, sits on a mountain of coal. He is smiling at his brothers.*

TOM: We'll be warm for the whole winter, Christy.

EXT. CHRISTY'S HOUSE. DAY

MRS BROWN *answers the door and gets a shock when all she can see of* CHRISTY *is two white eyes and a set of teeth.*

MRS BROWN: Oh! Jesus, Mary and Joseph. What happened to you?

TOM: It's all right, Ma, it's only coal.

MRS BROWN: Where did you get that coal?

(CHRISTY *mutters something indecipherable again.* BENNY *starts to laugh.*)

TOM: What did Christy say?

BENNY: 'Off the back of a lorry.'

(TOM *laughs and looks at* CHRISTY *who looks totally demonic as he laughs outrageously, for the first time ever being the leader of the gang. He loves this position.* MRS BROWN *looks at him very seriously.*)

MRS BROWN: Christy Brown, don't you know stealing is a sin? Don't you know God's looking down on you? That coal is not coming into this house.

(*She shuts the door.*)

INT. LIVING ROOM. NIGHT

A huge coal fire blazes in the hearth. MRS BROWN *is in the kitchenette.*

MR BROWN: Come over and sit at the fire, woman.

MRS BROWN: That fire will bring nothing but bad luck to this house. I'm going up to bed.

(*After a moment* MR BROWN *follows her.*)

TOM: Let's read Christy's story.

(CHRISTY *is glum. They produce a tattered manuscript.*)

INT. LIVING ROOM. NIGHT

TOM: (*Reading*) Alone in bed young Sir Peter could hear the front gate imper–

(CHRISTY *growls.*)

– imperceptibly open and he could detect the noise of the club foot on the gravel. The great front door opens with a dull thud. It was too late now for young Sir Peter to cry for help. His parents were at the manor. On the stairs he heard the thump, thump, thump of the foot coming even closer.

(*Everybody is absorbed in the story.* CHRISTY *looks at his mother, who has her face turned away.* CHRISTY *is sad that his mother is not listening. Suddenly there is a noise in the grate. Everybody is too absorbed in the story to pay attention.* CHRISTY *starts to growl.*)

On the stairs Sir Peter heard the foot on the landing. He jumped from his bed and hid under it, his breath thumping in his chest.

(CHRISTY *is apoplectic by now, trying to get attention. He is pointing towards the fire. Suddenly he lets out the first phrase that we understand in the film.*)

CHRISTY: Ma. The fire. Fire!

(MRS BROWN *comes running. She reacts instantly and runs to the fire, withdrawing the silver box of money that has fallen into it. She takes the box from the fire without thinking and burns her hands but refuses to let the box go until she has deposited it on the floor. Then she puts her hands to her face and looks at them in agony.*)

MRS BROWN: Oh, Jesus, Mary and Joseph.

MR BROWN: Get water quick.
  (TOM *runs out for water.* MR BROWN *approaches* MRS
  BROWN *but only puts his hand on her shoulder.* TOM
  comes in with water in a container and MRS BROWN
  takes it and ever so gently pours it over the silver box.
  It cools down. Everybody looks at it and MRS BROWN
  leaves the room.)

INT. KITCHENETTE. NIGHT
MRS BROWN *cools her hands under the running tap.*

INT. FRONT ROOM. NIGHT
CHRISTY *and the family look at the box as they listen to the*
running water. MRS BROWN *comes back into the room.*
MR BROWN: What's in the box, woman?
MRS BROWN: Christy's money.
MR BROWN: What?
MRS BROWN: Christy's, for his wheelchair.
  (MR BROWN *goes over the box and opens it. Inside*
  there are several notes. He takes them out and counts
  them.)
MR BROWN: There's over twenty pounds here, woman.
MRS BROWN; There's twenty-eight pounds, seven and
  three.
MR BROWN: We're sitting here in the freezing cold eating
  porridge for breakfast, dinner and tea and you have
  twenty-eight pound, seven and three, up the fucking
  chimney.
  (*Close on:* CHRISTY, *trying not to be part of this.*)

INT. CHRISTY'S HOUSE. NIGHT
MRS BROWN *comes in with* SHEILA *and sits. The baby is in*
the Moses basket.
MRS BROWN: Get out of that, Tom, and let your sister sit
  down. Up to bed the lot of yous.
  (MR BROWN *reading his paper looks up over the top at*
  SHEILA. CHRISTY *leaves the room with the rest of*
  them.)
  Your daughter is getting married.
MR BROWN: That's wonderful news. When?

34

MRS BROWN: On Friday.

MR BROWN: What's the rush?

MRS BROWN: She's pregnant.

MR BROWN: That's fine, that's wonderful. That's all we need. Who is the father or do you know?

SHEILA: Leave me alone. It's not my fault.

MR BROWN: And whose is it, mine? (*Shouts*) Oh, by Jesus, yes, it's a lovely picture, the old woman who lived in the shoe and her daughter who couldn't keep her legs shut.

MRS BROWN: Stop it, stop it, stop it.

INT. CHILDREN'S BEDROOM. DAY

In the bedroom all the children are listening. Over the scene we hear the voice of the father.

MR BROWN: (*Out of shot*) We're rightly shanghaied now. Now I've two brood mares under me roof.
(CHRISTY *tries to finish the painting of hell. He is working on red wide eyes.* CHRISTY *has almost finished the painting. Downstairs he can hear the sound of furniture being thrown around and his father's voice raised in anger. Suddenly he can hear the words distinctly.*)
(*Out of shot*) Don't you answer your father back like that, you cheeky bitch.

INT. LANDING. NIGHT

SHEILA *flying up the stairs. The father comes up the stairs a few steps and stops. He turns his back and slumps down on a step. He puts his hands over his head.*

MR BROWN: Oh, Jesus, Mary and holy Saint Joseph. How am I going to survive?

INT. CHILDREN'S BEDROOM. NIGHT

SHEILA *comes into the room. The sight of eleven kids looking at this sudden woman is ominous.* CHRISTY *notices her black eye. He grunts.*

SHEILA: It's nothing, Christy.
(CHRISTY *growls and we can make out 'Kill him.' He makes towards the door.*)
Christy, don't, please. Tom, Benny, stop him.

(*The boys try to stop* CHRISTY. *He kicks them off with his ferocious foot, sending them flying.*)

Christy, please, for my sake, stop.

(CHRISTY *growls like a hyena.*)

Please, Christy.

(CHRISTY *howls again.* SHEILA *begs him to stop. At the bottom of the stairs the father's voice booms out.*)

MR BROWN: (*Out of shot*) Keep quiet before I come up the stairs.

(SHEILA *begs* CHRISTY.)

SHEILA: Christy!

(CHRISTY *stops, we are unsure why. He smiles and cries at the same time.* SHEILA *puts her arm round him.*)

I'm going to miss you, Christy. Brendan is taking me to England. Look after Mummy for me, won't you? You're the only one who understands, Christy.

INT. WELLINGTON ROOM. NIGHT

We hear the sound of applause. MARY *looks up at the Tannoy and quickly closes the book.* CHRISTY *makes an elaborate game of 'waking up'. He yawns.*

MARY: Did you have a good sleep?

CHRISTY: Beautiful. I had a dream.

MARY: What was it about?

CHRISTY: You. Who else?

(MARY *looks at him. There is a moment of tension. The door opens and several performers come into the Wellington Room.* MARY *watches eagerly to see who is who.* DR COLE *leads* LORD CASTLEWELLAND *and the Browns into the room. A servant carries in a huge tray of champagne. All the guests take a glass. Christy's brothers decline, which only serves to make things more awkward.* LORD CASTLEWELLAND *comes through the door and smiles at* CHRISTY. *He is followed by a servant with a tray piled high with Guinness. Christy's brothers hesitate and then* BENNY *steps forward. In two seconds flat the tray is emptied. A second tray with three glasses of Guinness appears and Christy's mother takes a glass.* CHRISTY *laughs.*)

(*Shouts*) Show my mother your clock.

(LORD CASTLEWELLAND *nods at* CHRISTY.)

INT. STAIRS/LOBBY. DAY
LORD CASTLEWELLAND *winds up his elaborate clock, showing*
MRS BROWN *how the winding works.*

INT. WELLINGTON ROOM. DAY
The PUNCH AND JUDY MAN *is showing the guests how the*
swazzle works, his voice high and shrill. CHRISTY *watches*
the performance, a wry smile on his face. The PUNCH AND
JUDY MAN *takes the swazzle from his mouth and speaks*
normally.
PUNCH AND JUDY MAN: I'm parched with the thirst.

EXT. GROUNDS. DAY
In the distance what looks like a slide. From the point
of view of a toddler we see LORD CASTLEWELLAND
appear at the top. He moves on to the slide and shouts as he
descends.
LORD CASTLEWELLAND: That's the way to do it.
    (*Christy's brothers laugh at* LORD CASTLEWELLAND'*s*
    antics as they drink their pints of stout. Somehow the
    drinks in their hands make them incongruous but relaxed.
    They almost look at home.)

INT. WELLINGTON ROOM. DAY
CHRISTY *watches a clown remove make-up and become*
normal.

INT. WELLINGTON ROOM. NIGHT
All the guests are gone.
CHRISTY: Give me a drink, for Jesus' sake.
    (MARY *pours* CHRISTY *a drink and gets a straw for*
    him. He gulps it down.)
MARY: Would you like me to loosen your dicky bow for
    you?
CHRISTY: Yes.
MARY: Don't worry, Christy, your book is beautiful.
CHRISTY: It's not bad. (*He means that.*) Do you know what
    I was going to call it?
MARY: What?
CHRISTY: *The Reminiscences* . . . (*He takes a drink, unable*
    to finish.)

MARY: *Reminiscences.*

CHRISTY: . . . *of a Mental Defective.*

MARY: That's a terrible title.

CHRISTY: It was my blue period.

MARY: You typed all of this with your left foot?

CHRISTY: I didn't do it with my (*Slight pause*) nose.

MARY: It's brilliant. I really want to finish it.

CHRISTY: Won't you hear it read later?

MARY: I have an appointment, I told you.

CHRISTY: Is he good-looking?

MARY: Who?

CHRISTY: Your appointment?

MARY: Who said it's a man?

CHRISTY: I don't care. You can meet who you like. (*Pause.*)
Is he?

MARY: What?

CHRISTY: Good-looking.

MARY: In his own way. (*Pause.*) He's nice.

CHRISTY: Do you love him?

MARY: You're very bloody nosy, Christy Brown.

CHRISTY: I was only asking. Would you like a drink?

MARY: Not when I'm working, I can't.

CHRISTY: Later.

MARY: I have a date, I told you.

CHRISTY: (*Lying*) I forgot.

MARY: You're a faster worker, aren't you?

CHRISTY: (*Gamey*) Ah, read your book.

MARY: (*Gamey*) I can't with you staring at me.

CHRISTY: I'll look away.

> (*He looks away.* MARY *laughs.*)

MARY: I really do want to read it.

CHRISTY: Well, go ahead.

> (MARY *looks at a picture of Eileen. Again the letters are
> spelt out* EILEEN.)

MARY: She's very pretty, isn't she?

CHRISTY: Prettier than that bloody picture.

> (*Close on: the painting of Eileen all pretty and blonde
> and classical.*)

INT. HOSPITAL. DAY

MRS BROWN *is sitting across from a* NURSE.

NURSE: (*On intercom*) Dr Cole, please. Hello, Eileen. Athetoid Cerebral Palsy. He's nineteen, yes.
(MRS BROWN *nods.*)
That's correct. I'll get his address, yes.
(*The* NURSE *opens a book displaying wheelchairs.*)
Dr Cole thinks this would be the best model for your son.
(MRS BROWN *looks and smiles.*)

INT. CHRISTY'S ROOM. DAY
CHRISTY *is behind an easel at the far end of the room painting. The walls are covered in paintings. Various stages of* CHRISTY's *development. What is evident from them is an extraordinary energy and a sharp line with strength of purpose. The painting* CHRISTY *is working on is surrealistic. An eye floats in the sky and various disembodied body parts appear in a circus-like setting. He looks at a collage he made where the words* CRIPPLE *and* PAINTER *occur several times. There is a ring at the door.*

INT. LIVING ROOM. DAY
MRS BROWN *shows a pretty woman Christy's scrapbook.*
MRS BROWN: That's the first painting Christy ever did. (*A numbers painting from a newspaper.*) He won a competition for that.
(*She flicks on. The paintings grow in style and ability. The painting he gave* RACHEL *is there, torn into pieces and then recomposed. On and on the paintings and newspaper articles go about* CHRISTY.)

INT. CHRISTY'S ROOM. DAY
CHRISTY *listens as footsteps ascend the stairs. All the time he paints. His mother and an attractive woman come in the door.*
MRS BROWN: Christy, this is Dr Cole.
DR COLE: Hello, Christy. You're a wonderful painter.
(CHRISTY *grunts thanks.*)
I'm a doctor, Christy, who specializes in cerebral palsy. We've just opened a clinic here in Dublin. Would you like to attend it?

(CHRISTY *grunts something indecipherable.* DR COLE
looks at MRS BROWN.)
MRS BROWN: He said we can't afford it.
DR COLE: We'll manage somehow. We have a rich patron,
Christy.
MRS BROWN: Well, Christy?
(CHRISTY *grunts a long sentence.* DR COLE *smiles at*
MRS BROWN.)
He said, 'Hope deferred maketh the heart sick'? What
does that mean, Christy?
DR COLE: I think I understand. You're coming to us very
late but we are willing to give it a go if you are.
(CHRISTY *grunts something.*)
MRS BROWN: He said that he'll think about it.

EXT. CHRISTY'S HOUSE. MORNING
An ambulance waits outside the door for CHRISTY. *He comes
out in his wheelchair. The* DRIVER *opens the back door and it
is full of young children, all of them handicapped in some
way.* CHRISTY *looks at them, appalled.*
CHRISTY: (*Decisive*) No.
(TOM, CHRISTY'*s brother, is there. He is now a good-
looking man of twenty.*)
TOM: You have to, you want him to tow you behind?
DRIVER: Sure, he can come up front with me.

EXT. CHRISTY'S HOUSE. MORNING
MRS BROWN, *afraid to come out, watches from behind a
curtain.*

EXT. CHRISTY'S HOUSE. MORNING
TOM *lifts* CHRISTY *to the front of the ambulance and the*
DRIVER *puts his wheelchair in the back with the other
kids.*

INT. AMBULANCE. MORNING
The ambulance drives through the country.

INT. CLINIC. MORNING
*A hand moves a curtain. Below we can see the ambulance
arrive.*

EXT. CLINIC. MORNING
Close on: the face of LORD CASTLEWELLAND. *As the door
of the ambulance opens he lets the curtain drop.*

EXT. CLINIC. MORNING
The ambulance pulls to a halt. The DRIVER *gets out
and opens the doors. He gets a girl's wheelchair out on to
the pavement, then lifts the girl out into it. Several
attendants lift the other kids out. Then they lift* CHRISTY
*on to the pavement. They bring his wheelchair round
and he sits in it.*

INT. CLINIC. MORNING
The DRIVER *wheels* CHRISTY *along a corridor, the wheels
creaking all the way. They come to a door. The voices of
children can be heard – laughing and crying. The* DRIVER
opens the door and wheels CHRISTY *into a big room.*

INT. CLINIC: LARGE ROOM. MORNING
To CHRISTY *it seems as if he's walked into a wall of noise.*
CHRISTY *is horrified, unable to watch, children of all ages,
with crooked limbs, distorted bodies, etc., squirm, wriggle,
move all over the floor crying, laughing or shouting. The*
DRIVER *goes out, leaving* CHRISTY *on his own.* CHRISTY *sees*
DR COLE *working with a child.* DR COLE *comes over and
talks to him.*
DR COLE: Don't worry, Christy, you'll get used to it.
    (CHRISTY *shakes his head to say, 'No.'*)
CHRISTY: Twake me woot.
DR COLE: We want you to try and crawl. Do you think
    you can do that, Christy?
    (CHRISTY *grunts, 'No.'*)
    Why not, Christy?
    (CHRISTY *grunts again.*)
    Just try, for my sake.
    (*We see* CHRISTY *struggle, crawling on his belly past
    deformed children.*)

INT. CHRISTY'S HOUSE. DAY
MR BROWN *comes in from work. He puts down his tools.*
TOM *follows him in, followed by* BENNY *and then* BRIAN. *All*

41

work the building sites. MRS BROWN *puts their dinners on the table.*

TOM: How's the painting going, Christy?
  (CHRISTY *grunts, 'Good.'*)
MRS BROWN: There was a letter from England today. Your daughter is after giving birth to another baby girl.
MR BROWN: She wouldn't be her mother's daughter if she didn't.
MRS BROWN: She sent a few photos.
  (*All look at the photos. The father with feigned uninterest.*)
TOM: Don't the kids look great? I might be tying the knot myself soon.
  (MR BROWN *looks at him as if he is mad.*)

INT. CHRISTY'S ROOM. DAY
CHRISTY *hears* DR COLE's *voice at the door. He stops painting and looks alarmed. He moves down from the wheelchair over to the door and, with his left foot, locks it.*

INT. STAIRS. DAY
MRS BROWN *and* DR COLE *are coming up the stairs.*

INT. CHRISTY'S ROOM. DAY
MRS BROWN *knocks on Christy's door.*
MRS BROWN: There's someone here to see you, Christy.
  (CHRISTY *grunts, 'Go away' from the far side. Then he grunts again.*)
  He says the children are too sad.
DR COLE: Fine, we'll work here. Christy, I think I may be able to help you. You will never walk properly but I think I can help you with your speech.
  (CHRISTY *grunts, 'Fuck off.'*)
  With speech therapy you will be able to say 'fuck off' more clearly.
  (MRS BROWN *is shocked.*)

INT. CHRISTY'S ROOM. DAY
Inside CHRISTY *starts laughing to himself. He opens the door with his foot. He grunts something.*

DR COLE: Nothing's hopeless, Christy, if you'll just
    persevere.

INT. LIVING ROOM. DAY
CHRISTY *sits at a table in the living room. He is trying to*
blow water through a pipe, from one bottle to another. The
bottles are connected by the tube and he has to blow the
water, which is coloured red, from the full bottle to the empty
one. He huffs and puffs but finds it hard to move the water.
DR COLE *watches him struggling.*
DR COLE: Your lungs are too weak. Try this instead.
    (*She gets a tin box with soapy water in it. She dips a*
    ring with a handle on it into the water. She holds it in
    front of her lips and blows. Bubbles fly everywhere.
    CHRISTY *smiles.*)
    (*Holding the ring to his lips*) Now you try.
    (CHRISTY *blows but his breath is misdirected.*)
    Try again. Big breath. Come on. Breathe in. Now.
    (CHRISTY *blows and the bubbles flow out. He's*
    pleased. They repeat the exercise and CHRISTY
    starts humming/singing 'I'm forever blowing
    bubbles'.)

CHRISTY: (*Singing*) 'I'm for'ver 'owin' 'ubbles . . .'
DR COLE: Take is easy. Take your time, Christy.
(*He blows a stream of bubbles.*)
Splendid.
CHRISTY: Ehsasillyord – plenid.
DR COLE: Pardon? Slowly.
CHRISTY: It's–a–silly–word . . . splendid.
(DR COLE *laughs. His mother looks in at the scene,
worried.*)

INT. CHRISTY'S ROOM. DAY
CHRISTY *is painting when his young sister* SHARON *runs into
the room, followed by* ALBERT.
CHRISTY: Get to hell out of here. I'm trying to work. Out,
out, out.
MRS BROWN: (*Out of shot*) Come on down out of that and
leave Christy alone.
SHARON: It's our room too, Christy Brown.
CHRISTY: Out! (*He flings the palette at her.*)

INT. CHRISTY'S ROOM. DAY
CHRISTY *is under the bed covers.* DR COLE *comes into the
room. She goes over towards the bed.*
DR COLE: Christy.
CHRISTY: (*Trying hard to be understood*) Leave me alone.
DR COLE: At least I can understand that.
CHRISTY: I want to be on my own.
DR COLE: It's only natural that you should be depressed.
That's a stage you have to go through, Christy.
Everybody gets depressed.
CHRISTY: You can get up and walk away.
DR COLE: Nobody can walk away from themselves, Christy.
If you want me to leave you alone I will. Do you
want me to leave you alone?
(*She waits awhile. No answer – she goes.*)

INT. CHRISTY'S ROOM. DAY
DR COLE *comes into the room. She brings* CHRISTY *a book.
He is still under the bedclothes.*
DR COLE: I've brought you a Christmas present.
CHRISTY: Thanks.
(*Pause.*)

44

DR COLE: It's the Collected Works of William Shakespeare. There is a speech in there I want you to practise. 'To do or not to be.' *Hamlet*. Stop feeling so sorry for yourself, Christy. Will you learn it for me, Christy? Look, I don't want to be a failure either, Christy. Will you try and learn it?

CHRISTY: Maybe.

(*She goes. After a while* CHRISTY'*s foot reaches out and takes the book under the covers. On the easel the painting is of Eileen Cole.*)

INT. LIVING ROOM. DAY

MRS BROWN *is ironing. Upstairs she hears* CHRISTY *trying to say 'To be or not to be'. He is having great difficulty. She listens for a while. He stops and then tries again. This time he keeps trying 'To be or not to be' and he is improving a lot.*

INT. CHRISTY'S ROOM. DAY

CHRISTY *is in his room trying to do his exercises. All the time he is reciting 'To be or not to be'. On the easel is another picture of Eileen Cole, this one more idealized and better executed than the first so that she looks like a Wyeth painting of Olga. On the floor* CHRISTY *stops for a moment and looks at another painting of Eileen. He then gets a brush and puts it between his teeth and finishes the blue in her eyes.*

INT. KITCHEN. DUSK

Upstairs the mother listens to CHRISTY *saying 'To be or not to be'. He has improved drastically. The steam from a new geyser floats upwards.*

INT. CHRISTY'S ROOM. NIGHT

CHRISTY: . . . that is the question. Whether 'tis nobler in the mind . . .

(*He looks up at the bunk bed above him. On the underside of the bed is the painting of Eileen Cole with a whole constellation drawn round her in illuminated ink.*)

INT. KITCHENETTE. NIGHT

MR BROWN *comes into the house and puts down his tools.*

Upstairs CHRISTY *can again be heard pattering away 'To be or not to be'.*

MR BROWN: That is the question. Whether 'tis nobler in the mind, to fucking suffer listening to that.
(*Pause.*)

MRS BROWN: He's in love with this girl Eileen.

MR BROWN: As long as he's getting better.

MRS BROWN: He could get hurt, Paddy. A broken body is nothing to a broken heart.

INT. CHRISTY'S ROOM. NIGHT

CHRISTY: (*Slow but more distinct*) . . . and by a sleep to say we end
The heartache and the thousand natural shocks
That flesh is heir to: 'tis a consummation
Devoutly to be wished. To die, to sleep;
No more.
(*During this speech night falls. On the underside of the bunk, from* CHRISTY's *perspective, a whole constellation has lit up. Sun, moon and stars.*)

INT. CHRISTY'S ROOM. DAY

CHRISTY *is sitting at his easel. He hears the voice of* DR COLE *downstairs and quickly collects all the paintings of her. With his left foot he raises the bedclothes and stuffs the paintings under it.* DR COLE *comes into the room.*

DR COLE: Great news, Christy. I told you about Peter's gallery. Well, he's given you your own exhibition. What do you think, Christy?

CHRISTY: I think you're brilliant.

DR COLE: I'm only as good as my patients.

INT. LIVING ROOM. DAY

MRS BROWN *and* MR BROWN *listen to* CHRISTY *and* DR COLE. MR BROWN *speaks the lines along with* CHRISTY.

CHRISTY: (*Out of shot*) And makes us rather bear those ills we have
Than fly to others that we know not of?

MR BROWN: She's working with him on a Saturday now?

MRS BROWN: She has to work with him on her day off. She's doing this voluntarily.

MR BROWN: She's a great girl altogether.

MRS BROWN: I wish we could afford to pay her .
MR BROWN: You were always from the other end of town, Maisie. You're getting it for nothing and you want to pay for it.
MRS BROWN: I have me pride as well as you, mister.
MR BROWN: I think you're jealous.
MRS BROWN: (*Considered*) Do you think that's our Christy up there?
MR BROWN: What do you mean?
MRS BROWN: Does that sound like our Christy?
MR BROWN: It sounds a lot better.
MRS BROWN: Not to me it doesn't.
MR BROWN: Are you fucking mad, woman? You can understand your son for the first time.
MRS BROWN: I always understood him.
MR BROWN: Nobody else did. At least he can function now.
MRS BROWN: That's not Christy's voice.
(MR BROWN *looks at her as if she's mad.*)
There's something about that voice that disturbs me.
MR BROWN: What do you mean, woman?
MRS BROWN: There's too much hope in it.
MR BROWN: What?
MRS BROWN: There's too much hope in it.

INT. CHRISTY'S ROOM. DAY
DR COLE: What do you think of Hamlet, Christy?
CHRISTY: (*Cocky*) No good. He's a cripple. Inside. He can't act.
DR COLE: He did in the end.
CHRISTY: Too late then.
DR COLE: Better late than never.
CHRISTY: Eileen, I like you very much.
DR COLE: (*Smiles*) And I like you, Christy. You have the heart of a poet.

INT. ART GALLERY. DAY
PETER: It gives me great pleasure to open this exhibition of the work of Christy Brown. A lot of people say Christy is a great crippled painter. That is an insult to Christy.
CHRISTY: (*Shouts*) That's right.

47

(DR COLE *holds his hand.* CHRISTY *looks up at her. His mother watches.*)

PETER: Christy is simply a great painter, full stop. He has struggled with his material in the same way that every painter must do to bring it under control. But it's not enough to have control.

(*As he speaks we pan around the paintings. All the familiar faces are there. There is a strange development in the paintings of* CHRISTY *himself. Going from a picture of honesty to one where Christy appears Christ-like and handsome. It is Dorian Gray in reverse.*)

(*Out of shot*) A great painter must also have inspiration and he must get that inspiration on the canvas with energy. As you look around the room today you see the forces that shaped Christy Brown. His mother and father and his brothers and sisters and the woman who brought him to public attention, Dr Eileen Cole.

(CHRISTY *applauds the mention of* DR COLE. *It is noticeable that he is drinking a lot of wine.*)

CHRISTY: (*Holding court*) There are only two kinds of painting, religious and the circus.

CRITIC: What's this?

CHRISTY: What do you think it is?

CRITIC: It looks like Jesus, Christy.

CHRISTY: It's a self-portrait.

(*Everybody laughs but* MRS BROWN *looks on, worried. She watches* PETER.)

Ma! Come here to me.

MRS BROWN: (*Sotto voce*) You're drinking too much, Christy.

CHRISTY: We're among friends, Ma, relax. We're going for a meal, Ma, you coming?

MRS BROWN: No, Christy, it's your day.

CHRISTY: I couldn't have done any of it but for you, Ma.

MRS BROWN: No, Christy, I better get your father home, he's not feeling well.

CHRISTY: No pints. Good wine.

MRS BROWN: Your father never drank anything but a pint in his life, Christy. I'll take him home. Will you get a taxi?

CHRISTY: Eileen is giving me a lift home.
MRS BROWN: I better be on my way so.

INT. RESTAURANT. NIGHT
CHRISTY: I think Mulcahy is a great painter. In here.
   (*Points to his chest.*) Soul.
PETER: I agree with Christy, Tony.
DR COLE: He's too way out for me.
   (*The waiter arrives with the wine. He holds it up.*)
PETER: Christy, try the wine.
CHRISTY: (*Holding glass aloft*) Intro ibo ad altare dei.
PETRA: What's he saying?
PETER: The Latin Mass.
CHRISTY: (*Coy*) I thought it was Joyce.
   (*Everybody laughs.*)
   The wine is A1.
PETRA: Can you tell which year it is, Christy?
CHRISTY: I'm not that sophisticated.
DR COLE: Not yet.
   (CHRISTY *gives her a knowing look. He drinks the wine
   through a straw in one gulp. Others watch, warily
   balanced between admiration and knowledge of bad
   manners.* DR COLE, *to break the embarrassment, smiles
   at* CHRISTY. *He smiles back.*)
CHRISTY: (*Sudden*) I love you, Eileen.
DR COLE: (*Embarrassed*) And I love you, Christy.
CHRISTY: No, I really love you.
   (DR COLE, *embarrassed, looks around. Close on:* PETER
   holding her hand under the table.)
   I love you all.
DR COLE: That's good, Christy.
CHRISTY: I even love (*pause*) Peter.
   (*He laughs out loud. Everybody laughs.* DR COLE
   relaxes.)
DR COLE: I'm glad you like Peter, Christy. (*Pretend secret*)
   Because we're going to be married in six months.
   (CHRISTY *is totally stunned. Silence. Embarrassment as
   he says nothing.*)
PETRA: What do you think of that, Christy?
CHRISTY: (*Trying to be relaxed*) Con . . . Con . . . (*Can't
   finish the word.*) Con . . .

(*He stops, breathless. His breathing is awkward. He
stammers and starts to throw his head back, his left foot
flashing up and down almost like an epileptic's. Finally
he gains control.*)
(*Fiercely*) Con . . . grat . . . u . . . lations, Peter
(*looking at* DR COLE *hard*) and Eileen on the won . . .
won . . . won . . . (*annoyed*) wonderful
news.
(*He stops. He doesn't mean a word of it and it is
obvious.*)
(*Smiling*) I'm glad you taught me to speak so I could
say that, Eileen.
TONY: Well, where were we?
PETER: Discussing Mulcahy.
CHRISTY: Mulcahy is empty.
PETER: I thought you said he was full of soul.
CHRISTY: I said he was empty. (*Shouts*) Whiskey.
(*The waiter comes over with the whiskey.*)
DR COLE: Take it easy, Christy.
CHRISTY: (*Deadly earnest*) You're not my mother. Never
forget that.
(*The waiter brings a whiskey.* CHRISTY *drains it through
the straw. Looks up.*)

I know what age that is. It's ten years old. The same
age as me.
TONY: (*To waiter*) Don't give him any more.
CHRISTY: (*In command*) Pour!
(*The waiter pours.*)
PETRA: Take that whiskey from him, Tony.
CHRISTY: Touch it and I'll kick you with my left
foot in the only part of your anatomy that's
animated.
DR COLE: Please stop, Christy.
CHRISTY: Why did you say you loved me?
DR COLE: I do love you, Christy.
CHRISTY: Ah, you mean platonic love. I've had nothing
but platonic love all my life. Know what I say? Fuck
Plato. Fuck all love that's not 100 per cent
commitment.
(*Silence.* DR COLE *is hurt and close to tears.*)
TONY: (*Gallant*) So you've changed your mind about
Mulcahy, Christy?
PETER: (*Stinging*) Christy is a genius, Tony. That's the
prerogative of genius, Tony.
CHRISTY: Don't want to be a genius. Want to be boring
and normal like you, Peter.
(*Silence.* CHRISTY *drinks whiskey through a straw.*)
Let's discuss nature.
TONY: Keep quiet, Christy.
CHRISTY: Whiskey.
(*The waiter comes over.* DR COLE *turns away.*)
PETER: Christy, I can't have you go any further.
CHRISTY: What are you going to do?
(PETER *walks behind the wheelchair.*)
PETER: I'm going to wheel you out of the restaurant.
(CHRISTY *looks at* DR COLE, *holds on to the table like a
baby.*)
CHRISTY: It's get rid of the cripple time, Eileen.
PETER: Out of here.
(*He pulls.* DR COLE *is amazed at Peter's action.*)
Where's the bloody brake on this thing?
DR COLE: (*Strong*) Peter, stop!
CHRISTY: Pull down the blinds, Peter.
DR COLE: (*Slow and deliberate*) Peter, stop!

(PETER *finds the brake, pulls* CHRISTY *back from the table, pulling down the tablecloth. He goes to wheel* CHRISTY *out in a fury.*)
(*Standing*) Peter, stop it. You bastard!
(PETER *stops, shocked.* CHRISTY *looks at him triumphantly. Without looking back* PETER *walks out of the restaurant.* CHRISTY *sits there and drops his head.* DR COLE *sits, puts her head back and takes a deep breath.* PETRA *lifts a glass and drinks, tears in her eyes.* TONY *shakes his head from side to side.* CHRISTY *looks like a cripple.*)

EXT. STREET. DAY
CHRISTY *sits in his wheelchair. The street slopes down to a main road.* CHRISTY *sees a bus go by along the main road. Then a car.* CHRISTY *moves the wheelchair with his body. The wheelchair gathers speed and hurtles down the hill towards the main road.* CHRISTY's *face is set – a mask of self-hatred. The wheelchair is getting closer to danger. The speed is increasing. The wind rushes through* CHRISTY's *hair. He tenses himself as he gets to the main road. The wheelchair hurtles across the road and crashes into a wall.* CHRISTY *is tossed out unhurt . . .* CHRISTY *lies on the ground, looking up at the sky. The wheels of the wheelchair spin aimlessly.*

EXT. STREET. DAY
From Christy's room over his shoulder out of the window we see his father cycle up to the house. MRS BROWN *is out calling the children.* MR BROWN *stops and looks at her. He smiles, raises his hand and touches her face. The only tender moment between husband and wife.*

INT. CHRISTY'S ROOM. DAY
CHRISTY *falls back on the bed.*

INT. CHRISTY'S ROOM. DAY
CHRISTY *is in the bedroom. He has a piece of paper between his toes. Slowly he opens the paper. Close on: a shining silver blade.* CHRISTY *tried to manipulate it between his toes. It cuts him a little, he winces. The blade falls. Again he picks it*

*up. Winces and then hardens his face. He raises his foot. We
see him try to align his shaking arm with his foot, attempting
to slit his wrist. He tries once but misses by a mile. It is not
clear whether he is afraid or uncoordinated. The blade slips
to the floor.* CHRISTY *starts to sob.*

INT. CHRISTY'S ROOM. DAY
*Close on: a piece of paper with the following words: 'All is
nothing = therefore nothing must end.' We notice red
splotches on the paper.* CHRISTY's *foot moves to the paper,
his toe red with blood, between his toes now a pencil. We see
the effort on his face as he writes. Hatred, anger and
determination combined.*

INT. WELLINGTON ROOM. DAY
Close on: CHRISTY's *face. Bearded. He looks at the ceiling.*

INT. WELLINGTON ROOM. DAY
MARY *looks at* CHRISTY. *Then she looks at the manuscript.
A picture of Christy's father, 'R.I.P.' written underneath. It
is a good likeness. The most accurate of Christy's paintings.
The painting, however, is incomplete.* CHRISTY *catches* MARY
looking at him and smiles at her. She smiles back.

INT. CHRISTY'S ROOM. MORNING
Close on: beside the bed empty stout bottles.
MRS BROWN: Get up out of bed, Christy Brown!
CHRISTY: I'm not well.
MRS BROWN: You've a hangover, that's all that's wrong
    with you.
CHRISTY: Leave me alone.
    (MRS BROWN *pulls the clothes off Christy's bed.*)
MRS BROWN: You're getting more like your father every
    day, all hard on the outside and all putty on the inside.
    It's in there (*points to her heart*), Christy Brown, that
    the battles are won, not in the pub pretending to be a
    big fellow for all the lads. If you're giving up, Christy
    Brown, I'm not!
    (*She leaves the room.* CHRISTY *lies there looking at the
    holy pictures. He hears a rhythmical noise. He gets off
    the bed.*)

53

CHRISTY: Oh, me poor head.

INT. LIVING ROOM. DAY
CHRISTY *makes his way across the room towards the back door. He looks out into the back yard.*

EXT. YARD. DAY
MRS BROWN *is marking out a square with pegs, string and hammer.*

INT. LIVING ROOM. DAY
CHRISTY *is mystified by what she is up to.*

EXT. YARD. DAY
MRS BROWN *now has a shovel and begins to dig a trench between the lines of string, and ignores* CHRISTY, *who she knows is watching.*

INT. LIVING ROOM. DAY
CHRISTY *can't live with his puzzlement any longer and pushes himself forward towards the back yard.*

EXT. YARD. DAY
CHRISTY: What do you think you're up to, Ma?
MRS BROWN: I'm building a room for you.
CHRISTY: Don't be mad, Ma.
MRS BROWN: If you have your own room, maybe you'll start painting again. (*Starts to cry.*) Christy Brown, you have my heart broken.
      (CHRISTY *is dumbstruck.*)
CHRISTY: I'm sorry, Ma.
MRS BROWN: Sometimes I think you are me heart. That's what I think, Christy. If I could give you my legs I would gladly take yours. What's wrong with you, Christy?

EXT. YARD. DUSK
CHRISTY: More water.
      (MRS BROWN *pours more water into the cement which* CHRISTY *is stirring with his trowel. He sloshes it around and seems happy for the first time in ages. In the background we can see the beginnings of four walls.*)

MR BROWN: What in the name of Jesus is going on here?

MRS BROWN: Me and Christy are building a room.

MR BROWN: And have you got planning permission?

MRS BROWN: From who?

MR BROWN: The authorities.

MRS BROWN: If we were to listen to the authorities, Christy
would be in a home for the mentally retarded.

MR BROWN: Jesus, woman, what way are you building
this? Tom, Brian, Benny, come out here. Will yous
look at this?
(*They all laugh.* CHRISTY *is disgusted.*)

TOM: You might be a great painter, Christy, but you'll
never be a brickie.
(*They all laugh like they were on the job. Men's
laughter.*)

MR BROWN: (*Foreman*) Right, trowels, plumbline, cement,
shovel, water. Let's get moving. Brown and Sons
Contractors are on the job and fuck the corporation
and planning permission.
(MRS BROWN *winks at* CHRISTY.)
Right. Now you three start over there. I'll start here
and I'll be inside having me tea when you're still
working.

BENNY *and* TOM: Never.

MR BROWN: Let's go.
(*He starts working feverishly. The boys also rush, trying
to beat him.*)

EXT. YARD. DAY
The boys are slightly ahead. MR BROWN *goes in to get some
water.*

MRS BROWN: Boys, let your father win.

ALL THREE: What?

MRS BROWN: He needs it, boys.

EXT. YARD. DAY
MR BROWN, *working feverishly, is well ahead.*

MRS BROWN: Take it easy, father.

MR BROWN: Take it easy. I never knew how to do that
and you of all people ought to know that. Hey, boys?
(*He winks and they all laugh.*)

EXT. YARD. DUSK
The shed is almost complete. MR BROWN *picks up the last of his bricks like a chalice.*
MR BROWN: There she goes. (*To Christy.*) They've a long
way to go to be better men than their father.
(*He goes in.*)
MRS BROWN: Well, Christy that's the nearest he'll ever
come to saying that he loves you.

EXT. YARD. DAY
TOM *starts rendering.*

INT. SHED. DAY
CHRISTY *and* MRS BROWN *are decorating the shed.*
MRS BROWN: We'll need a nice curtain for that window,
Christy.

EXT. STREET. DAY
CHRISTY *and* MRS BROWN *walk along the street. She is
pushing the wheelchair.* CHRISTY *is laden down with parcels.
He seems happy. So does his mother.*

INT. HALLWAY. DAY
Christy's mother opens the front door.
MRS BROWN: (*Calling*) Paddy!
(*No answer. She goes to the inside door. It will not
budge. She puts her shoulder to it. Nothing. She tries
hard, nothing. She comes out past* CHRISTY *and looks in
the window.*)
Jesus, Mary and holy St Joseph.
(CHRISTY *is worried and starts to fret.* MRS BROWN
*tries desperately to open the inside door calling, 'Paddy,
Paddy, Paddy' hysterically.* CHRISTY *flings himself on to
the ground and crawls to the door. He accelerates like
we have never seen him, moving like a wounded animal
on his one good foot.*)
It's your father, Christy. He's fallen. He's fallen.
(*She pushes the door. It won't budge.* CHRISTY *tries to
push the door with his back. His mother helps.* CHRISTY
pushes his foot against the stairs and starts to heave.)
CHRISTY: Leave me, Ma.

(*For the first time we see* CHRISTY's *elemental strength.
It is awesome, frightening and close to death in its fury.
It is* CHRISTY *literally trying to get his father off his
back, pushing with all his strength. The door edges open
and* MR BROWN *slowly and then all at once collapses on
the floor.* CHRISTY's *head lies right beside his father's.*)
MRS BROWN: Ah, Mother of God. Mother of God, Christy.
What am I going to do?
(MRS BROWN *lies down on top of her husband.* CHRISTY
*looks up. Ever so gently he raises his hand to touch her
face, hesitates and lets it drop.*)

INT. PUB. DAY
Close on: the Brown family. SHEILA *is with her husband and
two children.* TOM *is there with his wife, who has a baby in
her hands.* CHRISTY *is finishing 'You'll never walk alone'.
All the family are in mourning clothes but they are defiant
and join the last verse that* CHRISTY *sings with great gusto.*
CHRISTY *orders a round. For everybody.*
SHEILA: Go easy, Christy.
CHRISTY: It's me painting money. Drinks for everybody.
Give Magso a drink.
NEIGHBOUR: Fair play, Christy. Your oul fella will never be
dead.

SHEILA: How is Ma going to survive?

   (TOM *shrugs his shoulders.* CHRISTY *watches, annoyed.*)

CHRISTY: We'll manage. Stop all the worrying. Give us a
   song.

   (*The* NEIGHBOUR *starts to sing 'Kevin Barry'.*)

NEIGHBOUR: 'In Mountjoy Gaol one Sunday morning,
   High upon the gallows tree
   Kevin Barry gave his young life
   For the cause of liberty . . .'

CHRISTY: Ah, shut up!

NEIGHBOUR: 'Just a lad of eighteen summers,
   Yet how no one can deny . . .'

CHRISTY: (*Shouts*) Will you give over. Shut up.

   (*The* NEIGHBOUR *stops singing.*)

   I'm sick of martyrs. Dying for Ireland. It's all shit.

NEIGHBOUR: What's wrong with Kevin Barry?

CHRISTY: He's dead. Isn't that enough to be going on
   with?

NEIGHBOUR: He gave his life for Ireland.

CHRISTY: Who asked him to go to the trouble? Ireland
   will never be free. It's trapped in there (*Pointing to his
   head*).

NEIGHBOUR: Ireland will be free all right.

CHRISTY: Ireland is the sow that eats her farrow. Ireland
   is a prison. Ireland and freedom are total
   contradictions.

NEIGHBOUR: Ireland will be free quicker than you will
   walk.

   (*The tension in the bar is now high.* TOM *gets up to
   defend* CHRISTY.)

CHRISTY: No, Tom. Not after burying Da. No trouble.

   (*The* NEIGHBOUR *watches triumphant. He winks at
   several big pals. They all smile.*)

TOM: Big bleeding mouth.

   (TOM *is perplexed.*)

CHRISTY: It's all right, Tom. No trouble.

   (*Close on:* CHRISTY's *foot surreptitiously grabbing a
   stool. The* NEIGHBOUR *raises a pint to his head. Bang,
   the stool sent flying by* CHRISTY *knocks it out of his
   hand. The pub erupts in a frenzy of fighting.* CHRISTY
   is in the middle of it, sending bar stools and anything else

he can get his foot on flying in all directions. Suddenly a
man comes over and hits CHRISTY *a haymaker right*
between the eyes.)
MAN: I don't care if you're a cripple or not.
   (CHRISTY *kicks the* MAN *at the knee joint, which doubles*
   him in two. CHRISTY *grabs him around the neck with*
   his foot.)
CHRISTY: Tom! Tom!
   (TOM *sees the man caught by* CHRISTY, *comes over and*
   knocks him out. CHRISTY *lets him fall to the ground*
   with a smile on his face. CHRISTY *sees another*
   opportunity and grabs a bar stool. The BARMAN *gets*
   another part of it and a fierce tug-of-war ensues.
   CHRISTY *pulls the bar stool out of the* BARMAN'*s grasp.*
   He throws it into a glass mirror.)
BARMAN: That's it, Christy Brown, you're barred. Worse
   than your father any day of the week.
   (CHRISTY *looks in the shattered mirror. He looks very*
   like his father.)

INT. CHRISTY'S SHED. DAY
CHRISTY *watches his mother put the washing on a clothes*
horse near the fire. She picks up a pair of socks, looks at
them and put them back in the basket. She picks out a small
pair of trousers and hangs them on the line.

INT. CHRISTY'S SHED. DAY
CHRISTY *is painting the picture we saw earlier of his father. He*
is concentrated but worried. BENNY *appears over his shoulder.*
BENNY: That's good, Christy.
CHRISTY: No, it's not.
BENNY: Why not?
CHRISTY: He's not there. I've no eye.
BENNY: What?
CHRISTY: Eye. No good. Forget it. Not a painter.
BENNY: I think it's brilliant. It's the image of Da.
   (CHRISTY *is despondent.* BENNY *notices the suicide note*
   from earlier.)
   What's that, Christy? Sorry I asked.
CHRISTY: It's the only good thing I ever did, Benny. From
   the heart. Will you help me, Benny?

BENNY: Doing what?
CHRISTY: Writing. My own story.
BENNY: Sure.

INT. CHRISTY'S SHED. DUSK
CHRISTY *dictating to* BENNY.
MRS BROWN: You can't write all day, Christy.
CHRISTY: Have to finish this chapter.
MRS BROWN: I brought you some tca.
CHRISTY: Thanks.
  (*He continues to dictate furiously.*)

INT. CHRISTY'S SHED. NIGHT
BENNY: I have to go for a pint, Christy?
CHRISTY: I'm off the drink for ever.
BENNY: What?
CHRISTY: Until I finish the book anyway. Go on, I'll be
  OK.
  (*He picks up the pencil with his foot.*)

INT. CHRISTY'S SHED. DAY
MRS BROWN: There's a letter here from London for you.
CHRISTY: (*Eager*) Give me a look. (*Opens it expertly with
  his foot.*) They've accepted me book. There's a
  cheque.
MRS BROWN: How much, Christy?
CHRISTY: Not much.
  (*He puts it in his pocket. His mother is surprised.*)

INT. LIVING ROOM. DAY
CHRISTY *watches as* BENNY *puts his hand up the chimney.*
He takes down the silver box.
CHRISTY: Don't say anything to Ma.
BENNY: Eight hundred pounds.

INT. LIVING ROOM. NIGHT
CHRISTY *and his younger sisters and brothers sit around the
table,* MRS BROWN *serving them.*
CHRISTY: Is there no dessert?
MRS BROWN: Dessert? You must think money grows on
  trees, Christy Brown.

CHRISTY: Ah, Ma, get ice-cream.
  (CHRISTY *winks at* BENNY.)
ALL: Yeah, Ma. Get ice-cream. Get's something. We're
  starving.
MRS BROWN: I don't know, am I a fool or what?
  (*She goes to the fireplace and takes out the silver box.
  She sits down and opens it.*)
  Oh, my God. My Jesus. Holy God, what's this?
  (*All the kids shout in exultation.*)
ALL: That's Christy's money. Christy's money. Let's count
  it, Ma.
  (*They take the box and pour it out.*)

INT. LIVING ROOM. NIGHT
CHRISTY *and his mother alone. The money is piled on the
table. She holds the silver box in her lap.*
MRS BROWN: Eight hundred pounds, Christy, that's more
  than your poor father earned in a year. I can't keep it,
  son.
CHRISTY: Do. It's yours.
MRS BROWN: I can't.
CHRISTY: Da was a bricklayer, Ma, I'm a writer. Keep it.
MRS BROWN: What will I do with it?
CHRISTY: Buy yourself a dress and a new pair of shoes.

INT. CHRISTY'S SHED. DAY
CHRISTY *is sitting at an electric typewriter, typing away. He
has a beard. The door to the shed opens and his mother
enters.*
MRS BROWN: Christy, you've got a visitor.
  (DR COLE *appears in the door.*)
  I'll leave you two alone.
DR COLE: You look well.
CHRISTY: So do you.
DR COLE: Thanks.
CHRISTY: Sit down.
  (*The bed is the only place to sit.* DR COLE *does.*)
DR COLE: I won't stay long.
CHRISTY: Stay as long as you want.
DR COLE: I need you to do a favour for me.
CHRISTY: What is it?

DR COLE: A benefit for the clinic.

CHRISTY: Where?

DR COLE: Lord Castlewelland's.

CHRISTY: Him. He's mad. Posh?

DR COLE: Filthy rich. I know you hate appearing in public
but it's for a good cause.

CHRISTY: For the cripples.

DR COLE: (*Smiles*) For the cripples.

CHRISTY: I'll try to behave myself.
(*He smiles.*)

DR COLE: You won't be too upset, will you?

CHRISTY: I'll anaesthetize myself.

DR COLE: (*Serious*) Not too much, Christy.

INT. WELLINGTON ROOM. DAY
CHRISTY *looks at* MARY *for a long time. There is a knock at
the door.*

MARY: We have to get going, Christy.

CHRISTY: Well? Too much self-pity?

MARY: No! I think he's a lovely man and not in the least
sentimental.
(*She starts to wheel him out.*)

INT. ANTEROOM. DAY
Coming into orangery.

CHRISTY: Do you honestly think that?

MARY: Yes.

CHRISTY: Would you go out with him?

MARY: Certainly.
(*They are almost at the stage.*)

CHRISTY: You would go out with me?

MARY: I might. Keep quiet, he's talking about you.
(*We can now see* LORD CASTLEWELLAND.)

LORD CASTLEWELLAND: Ladies and gentlemen, I want to
introduce you to one of the most courageous men it
has been my privilege to meet.
(MARY *nudges* CHRISTY.)

CHRISTY: Stay with me for a couple of hours.
(*She shushes him quiet.*)

LORD CASTLEWELLAND: When Christy Brown was born
the doctors told his mother he would have a very

short life and that he would be little more than a
vegetable. Mary Brown refused to believe the doctors
and she always believed her son Christy would
overcome the handicap of cerebral palsy.

CHRISTY: Will you go out with me tonight?

MARY: I have an appointment tonight, Christy.

CHRISTY: Are you in love with him?

LORD CASTLEWELLAND: Here tonight, ladies and
gentlemen, is living proof of the indomitable courage of
man. Let me introduce Christy Brown – man of genius.

CHRISTY: Do you love him?
(MARY *is troubled. The door opens. The audience
applauds.*)

DR COLE: Let's go, Christy.

CHRISTY: Wait, please wait. (*Loud*) Don't treat me like a
cripple. Mary, say something.

MARY: I'll see you again some time, Christy.
(*She goes, almost crying.*)

CHRISTY: Come back, Mary. Wait for the end.

DR COLE: We have to go now, Christy.

CHRISTY: I want Mary back.

DR COLE: (*Appealing*) Christy!

CHRISTY: Take me out to the firing squad so.

INT. ORANGERY. DAY

DR COLE *wheels him out. The audience applause grows.*

CHRISTY *on stage is terrified.*

CHRISTY: Get me out of here.
(DR COLE *smiles at* CHRISTY. *He can't be heard with
the audience applause.* LORD CASTLEWELLAND *stills the
audience.* CHRISTY *is fuming.*)

DR COLE: Christy wants me to tell you all that he is happy
to be here tonight.

CHRISTY: (*Under his breath*) Bollocks.

LORD CASTLEWELLAND: Ladies and gentlemen, let me say
how honoured I am to give voice to the words of
Christy Brown. (*He reads*) 'I was born in the Rotunda
Hospital on June 5th, 1932.'

INT. WELLINGTON ROOM. DAY

MARY *looking at the Tannoy as she takes off her nurses's*

uniform. She listens.

INT. ORANGERY. DAY

LORD CASTLEWELLAND: 'There were nine children before
    me and twelve after me. Of this total of twenty-two,
    thirteen lived.'
    (MRS BROWN *is unperturbed by this. The camera lingers
    on* CHRISTY.)
    'It would not be true to say that I am no longer
    lonely. I have made myself articulate and understood
    to people in many parts of the world, and this is
    something we all wish to do whether we are crippled
    or not. Yet like everyone else I am acutely conscious
    sometimes of my own isolation even in the midst of
    people, and I often give up hope of ever being able to
    really communicate with them.'

INT. WELLINGTON ROOM. DAY

MARY, *putting on her coat, is halted by the sound of* LORD
CASTLEWELLAND's *voice coming over the Tannoy.*

LORD CASTLEWELLAND: 'It is not only the sort of isolation
    that every writer or artist must experience in the
    creative mood if he is to create anything at all. It is
    like a black cloud sweeping down on me unexpectedly,
    cutting me off from others, a sort of deaf-
    muteness.'

MRS BROWN: What's wrong with Christy?

INT. ANTEROOM. DAY

MARY *looks through the glass door towards* CHRISTY.
CHRISTY *has his head on his shoulder. For the first time he
looks like the dead Christ.*

INT. ORANGERY. DAY

LORD CASTLEWELLAND *reads out the last words of* My Left
Foot. *The audience bursts out in applause and then rises to
its feet to give* CHRISTY *a standing ovation. His mother just
sits there, overcome by the event.* TOM *nudges her and she
slowly rises to her feet. The press are snapping away, taking
pictures.* CHRISTY *is presented with a bunch of flowers. He
calls his mother to the stage. They bring the microphone over*

to him. He gives the bunch of flowers to his mother. Then he whispers something to her and she takes one of the flowers and gives it to CHRISTY.

INT. ORANGERY. DAY
CHRISTY *is signing copies of* My Left Foot *with his foot. The press are still taking pictures.*
CHRISTY: I've got writer's cramp in my foot.
  (*The chauffeur appears and joins* CHRISTY *and his family for a picture.* CHRISTY *calls to* MARY, *who is standing close by.*)
  Mary, come here, please.
  (MARY *comes over.*)
  Please take me over there.
  (MRS BROWN *watches* CHRISTY *and* MARY *talking, away from the main group.* CHRISTY *gives her the flower.*)
  I want to walk you home.
MARY: Don't you want to spend the evening with your family?
CHRISTY: I've spent the last twenty-eight years with my family.
MARY: What about your mother?
CHRISTY: My mother is happy when I'm happy.

EXT. CASTLE. DAY
We see CHRISTY *talking to* LORD CASTLEWELLAND. LORD CASTLEWELLAND *bends down to hear what* CHRISTY *has to say. He nods.*

EXT. CASTLE. DAY
Christy's brothers get into the car. The youngest of them, LIAM, *runs over to* CHRISTY.
LIAM: Are you not coming home with us in the car?
CHRISTY: No.
LIAM: You're mad, Christy, it's great.
CHRISTY: Get in the car before I kick your arse. Good night, Mother. Don't worry, I won't be too late home. Go on, go on, I'm OK.
  (*The first Rolls pulls out. Christy's mother goes to the second Rolls. The chauffeur opens the door for her.*)

MRS BROWN: Good night now, Christy.
CHRISTY: Good night, Ma.
TOM: Good night, Christy. Be careful, Christy.
CHRISTY: You're not me Da, Tom.
TOM: Be careful of him, Mary.
CHRISTY: Get in the car, Tom.
  (LORD CASTLEWELLAND *appears, carrying two bottles of champagne.*)
LORD CASTLEWELLAND: Last drinks now, please. Time's up, ladies and gents.
CHRISTY: Well done. I hope to see you again.
LORD CASTLEWELLAND: Yes, I hope to see you before closing time, Christy. Bye Bye.
CHRISTY: Well, just point me in the right direction and I'll take it from there.
  (MARY *turns the wheelchair and starts to push.*)

EXT. KILLINEY. DAY
CHRISTY *and* MARY *overlooking Killiney Bay. Many steep steps below.*
CHRISTY: A hundred and ninety-six steps to Shaw's Cottage.
MARY: How do you know?
CHRISTY: I was carried up them once.

EXT. HILL. DAWN
The dawn breaks over Dublin. CHRISTY *and* MARY *are at the Dublin mountains, watching the light break over Dublin. The birds are singing.*
MARY: How the hell did you get up that hill ahead of me?
CHRISTY: Every cripple has his own way of walking.

TYPEWRITER.
A foot appears on the screen and types the following with an electric typewriter: 'Christy Brown married Mary Carr. They lived together until his death in 1981.'